L. RON HUBBARD

SCIENTOLOGY: A NEW SLANT ON LIFE

Bridge
PUBLICATIONS, INC.

Bridge Publications, Inc.
4751 Fountain Avenue
Los Angeles, California 90029

ISBN 1-57318-037-8

I have been a successful actor for twenty-two years and Scientology has played a major role in that success. I have a wonderful child and a great marriage because I apply L. Ron Hubbard's technology to this area of my life. As a Scientologist I have the technology to handle life's problems and I have used this to help others in life as well. I would say that Scientology put me into the big time.

John Travolta
Actor

Scientology is such a key part of my life today that it really constitutes an approach to living that is optimum for me as an individual, as a member of a family, as a member of the groups I belong to, and as a citizen of the world.

Terry Jastrow
Emmy-Award Winning
Producer/Director ABC Sports

As a medical professional I am concerned with matters which deal with life. The knowledge about life which I have obtained from Scientology has been an incredible help to me. Being a Scientologist and knowing Scientology has allowed me to grow in compassion and understanding and has made me more effective in helping my patients, my children and others.

Megan Shields
Physician

I actually have gotten back a freedom from Scientology, a freedom to learn whatever I want to learn in life.

Chick Corea
Grammy-Award Winning
Jazz Musician and Composer

For the past twenty years Scientology has provided me and my family spiritual and intellectual growth which I thought unattainable. I highly recommend *Scientology: A New Slant On Life* to improve your life, your relationships and to gain true knowledge of who you really are.

Bob Adams
Former NFL Football Player

Scientology:
A New Slant on Life

IMPORTANT NOTE

In reading this book, be very certain you never go past a word you do not fully understand.

The only reason a person gives up a study or becomes confused or unable to learn is because he or she has gone past a word that was not understood.

The confusion or inability to grasp or learn comes AFTER a word that the person did not have defined and understood.

Have you ever had the experience of coming to the end of a page and realizing you didn't know what you had read? Well, somewhere earlier on that page you went past a word that you had no definition for or an incorrect definition for.

Here's an example. "It was found that when the crepuscule arrived the children were quieter and when it was not present, they were much livelier." You see what happens. You think you don't understand the whole idea, but the inability to understand came entirely from the one word you could not define, crepuscule, which means twilight or darkness.

It may not only be the new and unusual words that you will have to look up. Some commonly used words can often be misdefined and so cause confusion.

This datum about not going past an undefined word is the most important fact in the whole subject of study. Every subject you have taken up and abandoned had its words which you failed to get defined.

Therefore, in studying this book be very, very certain you never go past a word you do not fully understand. If the material becomes confusing or you can't seem to grasp it, there will be a word just earlier that you have not understood. Don't go any further, but go back to BEFORE you got into trouble, find the misunderstood word and get it defined.

DEFINITIONS

As an aid to the reader, words most likely to be misunderstood have been defined in footnotes the first time they occur in the text. Words sometimes have several meanings. The footnote definitions in this book only give the meaning that the word has as it is used in the text. Other definitions for the word can be found in a dictionary.

A glossary including all the footnote definitions is at the back of this book.

"The human mind

is capable of resolving

the problem of the human mind."

L. Ron Hubbard

CONTENTS

CONTENTS

INTRODUCTION

Who are you anyway? Where do you come from? What will happen to you? Are you a product of the mud as you have been told, to exist for a few years and then wither away and fertilize the earth from which they said you came?

Or are you something better, something finer? What are your goals? Where are you going? Why are you here? What are you?

Scientology has answers to those questions, good answers that are true, answers that work for you. For the subject matter of Scientology is you.

L. Ron Hubbard

1 Is It Possible to Be Happy?

1

IS IT POSSIBLE TO BE HAPPY?

Is it possible to be happy?

A great many people wonder whether or not happiness even *exists* in this modern, rushing world. Very often an individual can have a million dollars, he can have everything his heart apparently desires, and is still unhappy. We take the case of somebody who has worked all his life; he has worked hard and he has raised a big family. He has looked forward to that time in his life when he, at last, can retire and be happy and be cheerful and have lots of time to do all the things he has wanted to do. And then we see him after he has retired—and is he happy? No. He's sitting there thinking about the good old days when he was working hard.

Our main problem in life is happiness, but I'll tell you more in a moment. The world may or may not be designed to be a happy one. It may or may not be possible for you to be happy in this world, and yet nearly all of us have a goal to be happy and cheerful about existence.

You know, very often we look around at the world around us and say that nobody could be happy in this place. We look at the dirty dishes in the sink and the car needing a coat of paint and at the fact that we need a new gas heater, we need a new coat, we need new shoes or we would just like to have better shoes; and so, how could anyone possibly be happy when actually he can't have everything he wants? He is unable to do all the things he'd like to do, and therefore, this environment doesn't permit a person to be as happy as he could be. Well, I'll tell you a funny thing—a lot of philosophers have said this many, many times—but the truth of the matter is that all the happiness *you* ever find lies in *you*.

You remember when you were maybe five years old, and you went out in the morning and you looked at the day, and it was a very, very beautiful day, and you looked at the flowers and they were *very* beautiful flowers. Twenty-five years later you get up in the morning, you take a look at the flowers—they are wilted. The day isn't a happy day. Well, what has changed? You know they are the same flowers, it's the same world, something must have changed. Probably it was you.

Actually, a little child derives all of his pleasure in life from the grace he puts upon life. He waves a magic hand and brings all manner of interesting things into being out in the society. Here is this big, strong brute of a man riding his iron steed,[1] up and down, and boy, he'd like to be a cop. Yes sir! He would sure like to be a cop; and twenty-five years later he looks at that cop riding up and down and checks his speedometer and says, "Doggone these cops!"

Well, what is changed here? Has the cop changed? No. Just the attitude toward him. One's attitude toward life makes every possible difference in one's living. You know you don't have to study a thousand ancient books

1. **iron steed:** figuratively, a motorcycle.

to discover that fact. But sometimes it needs to be pointed out again that *life* doesn't change so much as *you.*

Once upon a time, perhaps, you were thinking of being married and having a nice home and having a nice family; everything would be just fine. The husband would come home and you would put the dinner on the table and everybody would be happy about the whole thing; and then you got married and maybe it didn't quite work out. Somehow or other, he comes home late and he has had an argument with the boss, and he doesn't feel well. He doesn't want to go to the movies and he doesn't see how you have any work to do anyhow—after all, you sit home all day and do nothing—and you know he doesn't do any work either. He disappears out of the house. He's gone. Then he comes back later in the evening and quite an argument could ensue over this. Actually, both of you work quite hard. Well, what do we do with a condition like this? Do we just break up the marriage? Or touch a match to the whole house? Or throw the kids in the garbage can? Or go home to Mother? Or what do we do?

Well, there are many, many things we could do, and the least of them is to take a look at the environment. You know, just look around and say, "Where am I? What am I doing here?" And then, once you have found out where you are, why, try to find out how you can make that a little more habitable. The day when you stop building your own environment, when you stop building your own surroundings, when you stop waving a magic hand and gracing everything around you with magic and beauty, things cease to be magical, things cease to be beautiful.

Other people seek happiness in various ways. They seek it hectically, as though it's some sort of mechanism that exists. Maybe it's a little machine, maybe it's parked in the cupboard, maybe happiness is down at the next corner or maybe it's someplace else. They're looking for something, but the odd part of it is, the only time they ever find something is when they put it there first. Now, this doesn't seem very creditable, but it's quite true. Those people who have become unhappy about life *are* unhappy about life solely and completely because life has ceased to be made by them. Here we have the single difference in a human being. We have here a human being who is unhappy, miserable and isn't getting along in life, who is sick, who doesn't see brightness. Life is handling, running, changing, making him.

And here you have somebody who is happy, who is cheerful, who is strong, who finds that there is something worth doing in life, and what do we discover in this person? We find out that he is making life, and there is actually a single difference: Are *you* making life, or is life making *you*?

And when we go into this we find out that a person has stopped making life because he himself has decided that life cannot be made. Some failure, some small failure, maybe not graduating with the same class, or maybe that failure that had to do with not marrying quite the first man or woman that came along who seemed desirable, or maybe the failure of having lost a car, or just some minor thing in life started this attitude. A person looked around one day and said, "Well, I've lost," and after that life makes him, he doesn't make life anymore.

Now, this would be a very dreadful situation if nothing could be done about it, but the fact of the matter is that it is the easiest problem of all the problems man faces: changing himself and changing the attitudes of those around him. It is very, very easy to change somebody else's attitude. Yet, you are totally dependent upon other people's attitudes—somebody's attitude toward you may make or break your life. Did it ever occur to you that your home holds together probably because of the attitude the other person has toward you? So there are really two problems here—you would have to change two attitudes: (1) your attitude toward somebody else; and (2) their attitude toward you. Well, are there ways to do this? Yes, fortunately, there are.

For many, many centuries, man has desired to know how to change the mind and condition of himself and his fellows. Actually, man hadn't accumulated enough information to do this up to relatively few years ago. But we are making it a very fast-paced world, we are making it a world where magic is liable to occur at any time, and has.

Man now understands a great many things about the universe he lives in, which he never understood before. Amongst the things he now understands is the human mind. The human mind is not an unsolved problem.

Nineteenth-century psychology[2] didn't solve the problem, but that doesn't mean it has not been solved.

In modern times, the most interesting miracles are taking place all across this country and across other continents of Earth. What do these miracles consist of? They consist of people becoming well when they were ill, incurably ill. They consist of people who were unhappy becoming happy once more. They consist of abolishing the danger inherent in many of the illnesses and many of the conditions of man. Yet the answer has been with man all the time; man has been able to reach out and find this answer, so perhaps man himself had to change. Perhaps he had to come up to modern times to find out that the physical universe[3] was not composed of demons and ghosts, to outlive his superstitions, to outlive the ignorance of his forebears. Perhaps he had to do everything, including inventing the atom bomb, before he could finally find himself.

Well, he has pretty well mastered the physical universe now. The physical universe is, to him rather a pawn; he can do many things with it. And, having conquered that, he can now conquer himself. The truth of the matter is he *has* conquered himself. The religious philosophy of Scientology came about because of a man's increased knowledge of energy. Man became possessed of more information about energy than he had had

---

2. **psychology:** the study of the human brain and stimulus-response mechanisms. Its code word was: "Man, to be happy, must adjust to his environment." In other words, man, to be happy, must be a total effect.

3. **physical universe:** the universe of matter, energy, space and time. It would be the universe of the planets, their rocks, rivers and oceans, the universe of stars and galaxies, the universe of burning suns and time.

before in all of his history; and amongst that, he came into possession of information about the energy which is his own mind. The body *is* an energy mechanism. Naturally, a person who cannot handle energy could not handle a body. He would be tired, he would be upset, he would be unhappy, and he looks all around him to find nothing but energy. If he knew a great deal about energy, particularly the energy of himself and the space which surrounds him, he, of course, would know himself; and that, in the final essence,[4] has been his goal for many thousands of years. To know himself.

Scientology has made it possible for him to do so.

<hr>

4. in the final essence: essentially; at bottom, often despite appearances.

2 THE TRUE STORY OF SCIENTOLOGY

2

THE TRUE STORY OF SCIENTOLOGY

The true story of Scientology is simple, concise and direct. It is quickly told:

1. A philosopher develops a philosophy about life and death.

2. People find it interesting.

3. People find it works.

4. People pass it along to others.

5. It grows.

When we examine this extremely accurate and very brief account, we see that there must be in our civilization some very disturbing elements for anything else to be believed about Scientology.

These disturbing elements are the Merchants of Chaos. They deal in confusion and upset. Their daily bread is made by creating chaos. If chaos were to lessen, so would their incomes.

The politician, the reporter, the medico,[1] the drug manufacturer, the militarist[2] and arms manufacturer,

---

1. **medico:** a physician or surgeon; doctor.
2. **militarist:** a person who supports or advocates the policy of maintaining a large military establishment.

the police and the undertaker, to name the leaders of the list, fatten only upon "the dangerous environment." Even individuals and family members can be Merchants of Chaos.

It is to their interest to make the environment seem as threatening as possible, for only then can they profit. Their incomes, force and power rise in direct ratio to the amount of threat they can inject into the surroundings of the people. With that threat they can extort revenue, appropriations, heightened circulations and recompense without question. These are the Merchants of Chaos. If they did not generate it and buy and sell it, they would, they suppose, be poor.

For instance, we speak loosely of "good press." Is there any such thing today? Look over a newspaper. Is there anything *good* on the front page? Rather, there is murder and sudden death, disagreement and catastrophe. And even that, bad as it is, is sensationalized to make it seem worse.

This is the coldblooded manufacture of "a dangerous environment." People do not need this news; and if they did, they need the facts, not the upset. But if you hit a person hard enough, he can be made to give up money. That's the basic formula of extortion. That's the way papers are sold. The impact makes them stick.

A paper has to have chaos and confusion. A "news story" has to have "conflict," they say. So there is no good press. There is only *bad* press about everything. To yearn for "good press" is foolhardy in a society where the Merchants of Chaos reign.

Look what has to be done to the true story of Scientology in order to "make it a news story" by modern press standards. Conflict must be injected where there is none. Therefore the press has to dream up upset and conflict.

Let us take the first line. How does one make conflict out of it? No. 1, *A philosopher develops a philosophy about life and death.*

The Chaos Merchant *has* to inject one of several possible conflicts here: He is not a doctor of philosophy, they have to assert. They are never quite bold enough to say it is not a philosophy. But they can and do go on endlessly, as their purpose compels them, in an effort to invalidate[3] the identity of the person developing it.

In actual fact, the developer of the philosophy was very well grounded[4] in academic subjects and the humanities,[5] probably better grounded in formal philosophy alone than teachers of philosophy in universities.

The one-man effort is incredible in terms of study and research hours and is a record never approached in living memory, but this would not be considered newsworthy. To write the simple fact that a philosopher had developed a philosophy is not newspaper-type news and it would not disturb the environment. Hence, the elaborate news fictions about No. 1 above.

---

3. **invalidate:** refute or degrade or discredit or deny.
4. **well grounded:** having a thorough basic knowledge of.
5. **humanities:** the branches of learning concerned with human thought and relations, as distinguished from the sciences; especially literature, philosophy, history, etc.

Then take the second part of the true story: *People find it interesting.* It would be very odd if they didn't, as everyone asks these questions of himself and looks for the answers to his own beingness,[6] and the basic truth of the answers is observable in the conclusions of Scientology.

However, to make this "news" it has to be made disturbing. People are painted as kidnapped or hypnotized and dragged as unwilling victims up to read the books or listen.

The Chaos Merchant leaves No. 3 very thoroughly alone. It is dangerous ground for him. *People find it works.* No hint of workability would ever be attached to Scientology by the press, although there is no doubt in the press mind that *it* does work. That's why it's dangerous. It calms the environment. So any time spent trying to convince press that Scientology works is time spent upsetting a reporter.

On No. 4, *People pass it along to others,* the press feels betrayed. "Nobody should believe anything they don't read in the papers. How dare word of mouth[7] exist!" So, to try to stop people from listening, the Chaos Merchant has to use words like *cult.* That's "a closed group," whereas Scientology is the most open group on Earth to anyone. And they have to attack organizations and their people to try to keep people out of Scientology.

---

6. **beingness:** the assumption or choosing of a category of identity. Beingness is assumed by oneself or given to oneself or is attained. Examples of beingness would be one's own name, one's profession, one's physical characteristics, one's role in a game—each and all of these could be called one's beingness.
7. **word of mouth:** informal oral communication.

Now, as for No. 5, *It grows,* we have the true objection.

As truth goes forward, lies die. The slaughter of lies is an act that takes bread from the mouth of a Chaos Merchant. Unless he can lie with wild abandon about how bad it all is, he thinks he will starve.

The world simply must *not* be a better place according to the Chaos Merchant. If people were less disturbed, less beaten down by their environments, there would be no new appropriations for police and armies and big rockets and there'd be not even pennies for a screaming sensational press.

So long as politicians move upward on scandal, police get more pay for more crime, medicos get fatter on more sickness, there will be Merchants of Chaos. They're paid for it.

And their threat is the simple story of Scientology. For that is the true story. And behind its progress there is a calmer environment in which a man can live and feel better. If you don't believe it, just stop reading newspapers for two weeks, and see if you feel better. Suppose you had all such disturbances handled?

The pity of it is, of course, that even the Merchant of Chaos needs us, not to get fatter, but just to live himself as a being.

So the true story of Scientology is a simple story.

And too true to be turned aside.

❋

3 MAN'S SEARCH FOR HIS SOUL

3

MAN'S SEARCH FOR HIS SOUL

For countless ages past, man has been engaged upon a search.

All thinkers in all ages have contributed their opinion and considerations to it. No scientist, no philosopher, no leader has failed to comment upon it. Billions of men have died for one opinion or another on the subject of this search, and no civilization, mighty or poor, in ancient or in modern times, has endured without battle on its account.

The human soul, to the civilized and barbaric alike, has been an endless source of interest, attention, hate or adoration.

To say that I have found the answer to all riddles of the soul would be inaccurate and presumptuous.[1] To discount what I have come to know and to fail to make that known after observing its benefits would be a sin of omission against man.

After thirty-one years of inquiry and thought and after fifteen years of public activity wherein I observed the material at work and its results, I can announce that in the knowledge I have developed there must lie the answers to that riddle, to that enigma,[2] to that problem—the human

---

1. **presumptuous:** too bold or forward; taking too much for granted.
2. **enigma:** a perplexing, baffling or seemingly unexplainable matter, person, etc.

soul—for under my hands and others, I have seen the best in man rehabilitated.

From the time I discovered that a human being is not his body, and demonstrated that through Scientology auditing[3] an individual can attain certainty of his identity apart from that of the body, I have been, with some reluctance, out beyond any realm of the scientific known. Knowing this, I must face the fact that we have reached that merger point where science and religion meet, and we must now cease to pretend to deal with material goals alone.

We cannot deal in the realm of the human soul and ignore the fact. Man has too long pursued this search for its happy culmination here to be muffled by vague and scientific terms.

Religion, not science, has carried this search, this war, through the millennia.[4] Science has all but swallowed man with an ideology[5] which denies the soul, a symptom of the failure of science in that search.

One cannot now play traitor to the men of God who sought, these ages past, to bring man from the darkness.

We in Scientology belong in the ranks of the seekers after truth, not in the rear guard[6] of the makers of the atom bomb.

---

3. **auditing:** the application of Dianetics or Scientology processes and procedures to someone by a trained auditor. The exact definition of auditing is: The action of asking a person a question (which he can understand and answer), getting an answer to that question and acknowledging him for that answer.

4. **millennia:** periods of one thousand years.

5. **ideology:** the doctrines, opinions or way of thinking of an individual, class, etc.; specifically, the ideas on which a political, economic or social system is based.

6. **rear guard:** a part of an army or military force detached from the main body to bring up and guard the rear from surprise attack, especially in a retreat. Used figuratively.

However, science, too, has had its role in these endeavors; and nuclear physics,[7] whatever crime it does against man, may yet be redeemed by having been of aid in finding for man the soul of which science had all but deprived him.

No auditor[8] can easily close his eyes to the results he achieves today or fail to see them superior to the materialistic technologies he earlier used. For we can know, with all else we know, that the human soul, freed, is the only effective therapeutic agent that we have. But our goals, no matter our miracles with bodies today, exceed physical health and better men.

Scientology is the subject of knowing how to know. It has taught us that a man *is* his own immortal soul. And it gives us little choice but to announce to a world, no matter how it receives it, that nuclear physics and religion have joined hands and that we in Scientology perform those miracles for which man, through all his search, has hoped.

The individual may hate God or despise priests. He cannot ignore, however, the evidence that he is his own soul. Thus we have resolved our riddle and found the answer simple.

※

7. **nuclear physics:** that branch of physics (the science of relationships between matter and energy) which deals with atoms, their nuclear structure, and the behavior of nuclear particles.
8. **auditor:** a person trained and qualified in applying Dianetics and/or Scientology processes and procedures to individuals for their betterment; called an auditor because *auditor* means *one who listens*.

4 THE ARC TRIANGLE

4

THE ARC TRIANGLE

In Scientology we have a magic triangle—only we don't call it a magic triangle. It is just called ARC.

Life has three component parts: affinity, reality and communication. These form a triangle—A-R-C. They are interdependent to such a degree that if you interrupt any one of them, you will interrupt the flow of the other two.

Let us examine the component parts of this triangle.

The first corner is affinity. One could call it, sloppily, love, but that is hardly descriptive enough. Affinity is the sympathetic[1] coexistence of two things or two parts of the same energy.

When we take a tuning fork in the physical universe and strike it and it starts vibrating at its particular frequency,[2] another tuning fork with the same frequency will begin to vibrate too, though it has not been touched. If you damp the first one out, you find the other tuning fork is ringing. They are in the same level, so therefore you could say they have sympathetic[3] vibration.

---

1. **sympathetic:** in agreement; harmonious; in accord.
2. **frequency:** the number of times something is repeated in a certain period (i.e., a *frequency* of 1,000 vibrations per second).
3. **sympathetic:** *(physics)* noting or pertaining to vibrations, sounds, etc., produced by a body as the direct result of similar vibrations in a different body.

Two men talking with each other either are in affinity with each other or they aren't. If they are not, they will argue. If they are in affinity with each other, two other things have to be there: They have to have agreed upon a reality and they have to be able to communicate that reality to each other.

This brings us to the next corner: reality. When you speak of reality, physical-universe reality, it is a very interesting thing. There is really no such thing as the physical universe; there is a motion. But we sense something; we see something with our eyes, we hear something with our ears, we smell something with our nose, we touch something with our hands, and we decide, then, that there is something. But the only way we know it is through our senses and those senses are artificial channels. We are not in direct contact with the physical universe. We are in contact through our sense channels with it.

Those sense channels can be blunted. For instance, a man loses his eyesight, and as far as he is concerned there is no light or shape or color or depth perception to the physical universe. It still has a reality to him, but it is not the same reality as another person's. In other words, he is unable to conceive a physical universe completely without sight. One can't conceive these things without senses. So the physical universe is seen through these senses.

You and I can take a look at a table and agree it is a table. It is made out of wood, it is brown. We agree to that. Of course, you understand that when I say "brown" and you hear "brown," brown actually to you may be purple but you have agreed that it is brown because all your life people have been pointing to this color vibration and saying "brown." It might really be red to me, but I recognize it as brown. So we are in agreement although we might be seeing something different. But we agree this is brown, this is wood, this is a table. Now a fellow walks in the door, comes up and takes a look at this thing and says, "Huh! An elephant!"

You say, "It's a table, see? Elephants are . . ."

"No, it's an elephant."

So we say he is crazy. He doesn't agree with us. Do we attempt further to communicate with him? No. He doesn't agree with us. He has not agreed upon this reality. Are we in affinity with him? No. We say, "This guy is crazy." We don't like him. We don't want to be around him.

Now let's say you and I are arguing, and you say, "That table is made out of wood," and I say, "No, it is not. It's made out of metal which is painted to look like wood." We start arguing about this; we are trying to reach a point of agreement and we can't reach this point of agreement. Another fellow comes up and takes a look at the table and says, "As a matter of fact, the legs are painted to look like wood, but the top is wood and it is brown and it is a table." You and I then reach an agreement. We feel an affinity. All of a sudden we feel friendly and we feel friendly toward him. He solved the problem. We have reached an agreement and we go into communication.

The most important corner of the ARC triangle is communication. How do people go into communication with each other?

In order for there to be communication, there must be agreement and affinity. In order for there to be affinity, there must be agreement on reality and communication. In order for there to be reality and agreement, there must be affinity and communication—one, two, three. If you knock affinity out, communication and reality go. If you knock reality out, communication and affinity will go. If you knock communication out, they will all go.

There are several ways to block a communication line.[4] One is to cut it, another one is to make it so painful that the person receiving it will cut it, and another one is to put so much on it that it jams. Those are three very important things to know about a communication line. Also, that communication must be *good* communication: the necessary data sent in the necessary direction and received.

All that communication will be about, by the way, is reality and affinity concerning the physical universe. Discussions will be whether there is or is not affinity, or whether there is or is not agreement and where the agreement is particularly disagreed with on the physical universe.

Affinity can be built up in a number of ways. You can talk to people and build up an affinity with them. But remember this is communication, not just talk. There are many, many ways to communicate. Two

4. **communication line:** the route along which a communication travels from one person to another; the line on which particles flow; any sequences through which a message of any character may go.

people can sit and look at each other and be in communication. One of the ways to go into communication is by tactile. You can pet a cat, and the cat all of a sudden starts to purr; you are in communication with the cat. You can reach out and shake a person's hand and you are in communication with him because tactile has taken place. The old-school[5] boys with the tooth-and-claw[6] idea that "everybody hates everybody really, and everybody is on the defensive and that is why we have to force everybody into being social animals" said that the reason men shake hands is to show there is no weapon in the hand. No, it is a communication. In France, Italy, Spain and so forth they throw their arms around each other; there is lots of contact and that contact is communication.

If a person is badly out of communication and you reach out and pat him on the shoulder and he dodges slightly (he considers all things painful) even though he doesn't go on, you will find he is also out of communication vocally. You try to say something to him. "You know, I think that's a pretty good project, Project 342A, and I think we ought to go along with it." He will sit there and look at you and nod, and then he will go down and complete Project 36.

You say, "Project 36 has just been thrown out. We weren't going to go through with that at all," but he hardly knows you are talking to him. He dodges

---

5. **old-school:** (of or like) a group of people who cling to traditional or conservative ideas, methods, etc.

6. **tooth-and-claw:** characterized by the need of fighting *tooth and claw,* that is, fighting with great determination and effort (against someone or something).

everything you say. Or he may talk to you so hard and so long you don't get a chance to tell him you want to do Project 342A. That is dodging you, too. In other words, he is out of communication with you. Therefore his affinity is low and he won't agree with you either. But if you can get him into agreement, communication will pick up and affinity will pick up.

This is about the most important data I have ever run across in the field of interpersonal relations.

You can take any group of men working on a project and take one look at the foreman and the men and tell whether or not these people are in communication with one another. If they aren't, they are not working as a coordinated team. They are not in communication, perhaps, because they are not agreed on what they are doing.

All you have to do is take the group, put them together and say, "What are you guys doing?" You don't ask the foreman, you ask the whole group and the foreman, "What are you guys doing?"

One fellow says, "I'm earning forty dollars a week. That's what I'm doing." Another one says, "Well, I'm glad to get out of the house every day. The old woman's pretty pestiferous.[7]" Another one says, "As a matter of fact, I occasionally get to drive the truck over there and I like to drive the truck, and I'll put up with the rest of this stuff. I drive the truck, and I've got to work anyhow." Another man might say, if he were being honest, "I'm staying on this job because I hate this dog that

7. **pestiferous:** annoying; bothersome.

you've got here as a foreman. If I can devote my life to making him miserable, boy, that makes me happy. I really lead him a dog's life, too."

All the time you thought that those men thought they were grading a road. Not one of them thought they were grading a road. You thought they were building a road. Not one of them was building a road; not one of them was even grading.

This crew may be unhappy and inefficient, but you get them together and you say, "Well, you know, some day a lot of cars will go over this road. Maybe they'll wreck themselves occasionally and so forth, but a lot of cars will go over this road. You boys are building a road. It's a pretty hard job, but somebody's got to do it. A lot of people will thank you boys for having built this road. I know you don't care anything about that, but that's really what we are doing around here. Now, I'd like a few suggestions from you people about how we could build this road a little bit better." All of a sudden the whole crew is building a road. Affinity, reality and communication go right up.

The reason this works is that every point on the ARC triangle is dependent on the other two, and every two are dependent on one. One can't cut down one without cutting down the other two, and one can't rehabilitate one without rehabilitating the other two. On the positive side, one can rehabilitate any point on the triangle by rehabilitating any other point on it.

❧

5 TWO RULES FOR HAPPY LIVING

5

TWO RULES FOR
HAPPY LIVING

*O*ne:
Be able to experience anything.

Two: Cause only those things which others are able to experience easily.

Man has had many golden rules. The Buddhist rule of "Do unto others as you would have these others do unto you" has been repeated often in other religions. But such golden rules, while they served to advance man above the animal, resulted in no sure sanity, success or happiness. Such a golden rule gives only the cause-point,[1] or at best the reflexive effect-point.[2] This is a self-done-to-self thing and tends to put all on obsessive cause. It gives no thought to what one does about the things done to one by others not so indoctrinated.

How does one handle the evil things done to him? It is not told in the Buddhist rule. Many random answers resulted. Amongst them are the answers of Christian Science[3] (effects on self don't exist), the answers of early Christians (become a martyr), the answers of Christian ministers (condemn all sin). Such answers to effects

---

1. **cause-point:** the originator of something; the point from which something was begun or dreamed up.
2. **effect-point:** the receipt-point of an idea, particle or mass.
3. **Christian Science:** a church founded by Mary Baker Eddy (1821–1910), American religious leader, editor and author.

created on one bring about a somewhat less than sane state of mind—to say nothing of unhappiness.

After one's house has burned down and the family cremated, it is no great consolation to (1) pretend it didn't happen, (2) liken oneself to Job[4] or (3) condemn all arsonists.

So long as one fears or suffers from the effect of violence, one will have violence against him. When one *can* experience exactly what is being done to one, ah, magic, it does not happen!

How to be happy in this universe is a problem few prophets or sages have dared contemplate directly. We find them "handling" the problem of happiness by assuring us that man is doomed to suffering. They seek not to tell us how to be happy but how to endure being unhappy. Such casual assumption of the impossibility of happiness has led us to ignore any real examination of ways to be happy. Thus, we have floundered forward toward a negative goal—get rid of all the unhappiness on Earth and one would have a livable Earth. If one seeks to get rid of something continually, one admits continually he cannot confront[5] it—and thus everyone went downhill. Life became a dwindling spiral[6] of *more*

---

4. Job: the central character in the Book of Job, an ancient Indian work, later incorporated into the Bible. In this story, Job endures much suffering but does not lose his faith in God.

5. confront: face without flinching or avoiding. *Confront* is actually the ability to be there comfortably and perceive.

6. dwindling spiral: a phenomenon of ARC whereby when one breaks some affinity, a little bit of the reality goes down, and then communication goes down, which makes it impossible to get affinity as high as before; so a little bit more gets knocked off affinity, and then reality goes down, and then communication. This is the dwindling spiral in progress, until it hits the bottom—death—which is no affinity, no communication and no reality.

things we could not confront. And thus we went toward blindness and unhappiness.

To be happy, one only must be *able* to confront, which is to say, experience, those things that are.

Unhappiness is only this: the inability to confront that which is.

Hence, *(1) Be able to experience anything.*

The effect side of life deserves great consideration. The self-caused side also deserves examination.

To create only those effects which others could easily experience gives us a clean new rule of living. For if one does, then what might he do that he must withhold from others? There is no reason to withhold his own actions or regret them (same thing) if one's own actions are easily experienced by others.

This is a sweeping test (and definition) of good conduct—to do only those things which others can experience.

If you examine your life, you will find you are bothered only by those actions a person did which others were not able to receive. Hence a person's life can become a hodgepodge of violence withheld, which pulls in, then, the violence others caused.

The more actions a person emanated which could not be experienced by others, the worse a person's life became. Recognizing that he was bad cause or that there were too many bad causes already, a person ceased causing things—an unhappy state of being.

Pain, misemotion,[7] unconsciousness, insanity—all result from causing things others could not experience easily. The reach–withhold phenomenon is the basis of all these things. When one sought to reach in such a way as to make it impossible for another to experience, one did not reach, then, did he? To "reach" with a gun against a person who is unwilling to be shot is not to reach the person, but a protest. All *bad* reaches never reached. So there was no communication, and the end result was a withhold by the person reaching. This reach–withhold became at last, an inability to reach— therefore, low communication, low reality, low affinity.

Communication is one means of reaching others. So, if one is unable to reach, one's ability to communicate will be low; and reality will be low, because if one is unable to communicate, he won't really get to know about others; and with knowing little or nothing about others, one doesn't have any feeling about them either, thus one's affinity will be low. Affinity, reality and communication work together; and if one of these three is high, the other two will be also; but if one is low, so will the others be low.

---

7. **misemotion:** a coined word used in Dianetics and Scientology to mean an emotion or emotional reaction that is inappropriate to the present time situation. It is taken from *mis-* (wrong) + *emotion*. To say that a person was *misemotional* would indicate that the person did not display the emotion called for by the actual circumstances of the situation. Being misemotional would be synonymous with being irrational. One can fairly judge the rationality of any individual by the correctness of the emotion he displays in a given set of circumstances. To be joyful and happy when circumstances call for joy and happiness would be rational. To display grief without sufficient present time cause would be irrational.

All bad acts, then, are those acts which cannot be easily experienced at the target end.

On this definition, let us review our own "bad acts." Which ones *were* bad? Only those that could not be easily experienced by another were bad. Thus, *which* of society's favorite bad acts are bad? Acts of real violence resulting in pain, unconsciousness, insanity and heavy loss could at this time be considered bad. Well, what other acts of yours do you consider "bad"? The things which you have done which you could not easily, yourself, experience were bad. But the things which you have done which you, yourself, could have experienced, had they been done to you, were *not* bad. That certainly changes one's view of things!

There is no need to lead a violent life just to prove one can experience. The idea is not to *prove* one can experience, but to regain the *ability* to experience.

Thus, today, we have two golden rules for happiness:

1. Be able to experience anything; and

2. Cause only those things which others are able to experience easily.

Your reaction to these tells you how far you have yet to go.

And if you achieve these two golden rules, you would be one of the happiest and most successful people in this universe, for who could rule you with evil?

6 WHAT IS THE BASIC MYSTERY?

6

WHAT IS
THE BASIC MYSTERY?

In the general study of the world and its affairs, we find out the only way that you can make a slave—as if anybody would want one—would be to develop a tremendous amount of mystery about what it's all about, and then develop an overwhelming charge[1] on the mystery line. Not only develop a mystery, but then sell it real good; sell some bogus answer to the mystery.

Man is so used to this, that when you come along and put a perfectly good answer in his hands, why, he drops it like a hot potato. Because he knows what all answers are: All answers are carefully derived from mysteries with bogus answers, and all mysteries are going to cost you something sooner or later.

The development of the mystery itself stems from interpersonal relationships and man's general conflict with his fellows and his environment, and so on. And the basic mystery is—Who is he? There's no more basic mystery than that: "Who is that fellow over there?" That is the beginning of individuation,[2] of, not individualism, but *individuation*; of pulling back from everybody and saying, "I am me and they are them, and God knows what they're up to!" And then, after a while, the fellow takes it out of

---

1. **charge:** harmful energy or force accumulated and stored within the reactive mind, resulting from the conflicts and unpleasant experiences that a person has had. *See also* **reactive** in the glossary.
2. **individuation:** a withdrawal out of groups and into only self. The mechanics of individuation are, first, communication into and, then, refusal to communicate into.

the realm of mere blasphemy and puts it into worship. And he says, "Well, God knows what they're up to and he will protect me."

So what do we basically have? We basically have a mystery on who the other fellow is. Now, *science* originally meant "truth," and now it means research revenue. Science has so far abandoned the basic mystery, that they think there's a mystery on what is a floor, what is a ceiling, what is space! That is really a very cooked-up[3] mystery—because that floor and that ceiling and that space is what thee and me agreed to put there, and that's about all it is.

Wherever we have a mystery, we normally have a disagreement or a misunderstanding or an out-of-communicationness. And that's all there actually is to it, basically. A fellow had to disagree with whom he was looking at. He knew about it originally and he didn't want to know who that fellow was over there. He didn't want to know anything about the situation, because he had learned a lesson: If he communicated with it, he would be proved wrong!

So we had some people in our midst—you amongst them—who would put up a "this" and say it was a "that." And then you would get these things twisted somehow or another, and you'd say, "Why don't you communicate with *this?*" and then say, "You communicated with *that.*" After a while a fellow says, "Aw, I don't want to communicate with either one of them. Dickens with it.[4] Who cares what those things are. I don't want to know." And after that, he'd had it. He said, "I don't want to know," and therefore he had a mystery sitting across from him someplace. And he went

---

3. **cooked-up:** made-up; invented.
4. **dickens with it:** I don't care about it. *Dickens* is a word used instead of *devil* or *hell*.

so far along this line of not wanting to know that after a while he conceived that he didn't know. And then he went from there and said it's impossible to know.

Wherever man finds himself deeply instilled,[5] engrossed, surrounded with mystery, he is actually in conflict with himself and himself alone. That is why processing[6] works. *The only aberration*[7] *is denial of self.* Nobody else can do anything to *you* but *you.* That is a horrible state of affairs. You can do something to you, but it requires your postulate,[8] your agreement or your disagreement, before anything can happen to you. People have to agree to be ill; they have to agree to be stupid; they have to agree to be in mystery.

People are the victims of their own flinch. They are the victims of their own postulates, the victims of their own belief that they are inadequate.

An individual has to postulate into existence his own aberration, his own flinch, his own stupidity, his own lack of confidence and his own bad luck.

※

---

5. **instilled:** pervaded or inspired (with opinions, feelings, habits, etc.).
6. **processing:** the application of Dianetics and/or Scientology processes and procedures to individuals for their betterment. The exact definition of processing is: The action of asking a person a question (which he can understand and answer), getting an answer to that question and acknowledging him for that answer. Also called *auditing. See also* **process** in the glossary.
7. **aberration:** a departure from rational thought or behavior. It means basically to err, to make mistakes, or more specifically to have fixed ideas which are not true. The word is also used in its scientific sense. It means departure from a straight line. If a line should go from A to B, then if it is *aberrated* it would go from A to some other point, to some other point, to some other point, to some other point, to some other point, and finally arrive at B. Taken in its scientific sense, it would also mean the lack of straightness or to see crookedly as, for example, a man sees a horse but thinks he sees an elephant. Aberrated conduct would be wrong conduct, or conduct not supported by reason. Aberration is opposed to sanity, which would be its opposite. From the Latin, *aberrare,* to wander from; Latin, *ab,* away, *errare,* to wander.
8. **postulate:** a conclusion, decision or resolution made by the individual himself.

7 HAPPINESS AND INTEREST

7

Happiness
and
Interest

Dilettantism is supposed
to mean "good at many things." But one can extend
its meaning to "unprofessional at everything." A
dilettante is somebody who starts a savage run at
something, and is very enthusiastic at first. For
example, he is going to learn how to be a jet pilot.
Great enthusiasm. (Of course, dilettantes mainly
come into the field of the arts, but we will just
extend it to all of man's activities.) "Oh boy, am I
going to be a jet pilot. Oh man, am I going to be a
jet pilot!" Then the instructor says, "Well, here we
have to learn to do this and do that, and you have to
learn the army regulations and you have to learn
how to make a bed." Now he is not quite as enthusiastic as he was before.

He gets a lesson or two. Then the next thing you
know, he is out there at the commandant's office
asking to resign. Why is he asking to resign? What is
the highest common denominator to his activity, or
to the activities which cause these withdrawals from
life, activities, goals and enthusiasms? He has
erased all the interest in the whole subject of jet
pilots. He didn't have very much interest, he couldn't

mock it up.[1] He suddenly had come into a deposit of interest. He had been sold by a poster or something of the sort. This interest was very slight. He himself could not create interest. So he simply went into something and erased all the interest he had on the subject which left him with nothing but some attention which he had given to it before.

He is kind of stuck with it and feels rather soggy about the whole thing. But he is not interested in it anymore. Well, he gets out of that, and decides he is going to be a piano player. That is the thing to be— a piano player. He is very interested in being a piano player. He takes one lesson, two lessons, three lessons, and he meets a couple of other piano players. The next thing you know he is not even interested in the piano anymore. He quits, he is through. He doesn't take it up any further. He decides he is not so successful in that particular field and the best thing for him to do is to become something completely out of this world, something he is tremendously enthusiastic about: He is going to be a painter.

He gets to the point where he learns how to clean a brush and he quits. What has he quit for? This is a very important thing because any person

---

1. **mock (it) up:** create it. In Scientology, the word *mock-up* is used to mean, in essence, something which a person makes up himself. The term was derived from the World War II phrase for miniature models that were constructed to symbolize weapons (airplanes, ships, artillery, etc.) or areas of attack (hills, rivers, buildings, etc.) for use in planning a battle.

has quit just like this in various parts of life. He has quit time after time.

He is just as good, actually, as he ever was, yet his considerations have turned over so that he quits. The consideration is this: He can no longer create interest; he no longer runs on the interest which he himself generates.

He just takes somebody else's interest or a little bit of interest and he erases it before he gets into anything like hard work.

Believe me, it takes a lot of interest to get you through the task of digging half a mountain away to find some gold, or sawing down a redwood[2] tree. (And they didn't used to have saws when they first cut those things down; they had very bad axes.) It takes a lot of interest to keep a fellow at a job all the way through.

Interest is not at fault. It isn't because a person had become interested in things and then had been disabused[3] and betrayed and so had to withdraw from them. That is not what is wrong with the person. It is simply that he failed to keep on generating interest in what he was doing.

---

2. **redwood:** an evergreen tree of the California and southern Oregon coasts. It is among the world's largest trees, reaching a height of over 300 feet and an age of several thousand years.
3. **disabused:** *(in normal usage)* freed from false ideas; put right. Used here in the sense "robbed or deprived of."

There are an awful lot of people out there. They are looking for happiness.

Well, the clue to happiness is being interested in life. People's happiness is as great as they can create it. They will not experience happiness from any other quarter than their own generation.[4] They will get the amount of happiness that they can generate.

But this happiness is not itself an emotion. It is a word which states a condition and the anatomy of that condition is interest. Happiness, you could say, is the overcoming of not unknowable obstacles toward a known goal.

The anatomy back of it is simply this: how much interest can a person generate, and can he generate enough interest to get him over all the heavy energy which has to be invested along the line. It is how much interest he can generate himself, how much he himself can keep interested in life that makes him happy. Because happiness is application of self to existence. That is all there is to happiness.

So what happens to this dilettante? He doesn't create interest anymore, and you will find this individual looking for happiness. He is looking for happiness. Nobody else's happiness is going to be of

4. generation: the act or process of bringing into being; origination; production.

any use to him whatsoever. The only happiness he will ever get is from being able to create his own interest in things.

※

8 THE DYNAMICS OF EXISTENCE

8

THE DYNAMICS
OF EXISTENCE

very individual is made
up of a central thrust through existence. This drive, this
thrust through existence, is survival. It is the effort on
the part of the organism to survive.

We call the urge toward survival a *dynamic*.

As this urge becomes enturbulated[1] or influenced
by outside forces, it is either suppressed or it is alloyed[2]
with other people's purposes. That is to say, other
people force their purposes on the individual. In either
way, the dynamic itself becomes to some slight degree
enturbulated.

As the survival dynamic is cut back or as it is entered
or acted upon by other influences—other people and
the regular suppressors of life, such as the absence of
food, clothing and shelter—this dynamic can become
more and more enturbulated until it is headed toward
death, or succumb, exactly in the opposite direction.

The dynamic goes toward succumb in the exact
ratio that it is enturbulated. It goes toward survival in
the exact ratio that it is clean and clear.

That is regarding it as just one dynamic. If we take
a look at this dynamic through a magnifying glass, we

1. **enturbulated:** made turbulent or agitated and disturbed.
2. **alloyed:** weakened or spoiled by adding something that reduces value or
   pleasure.

find that in this one thrust there are actually eight thrusts, or *eight dynamics.*

The first dynamic is the dynamic of self. This would be man's urge toward survival for himself.

The second dynamic has two compartments: one is sex and the other is the rearing of children. This dynamic is man's urge toward survival as a future generation. On the first dynamic he is an individual. But by sex—procreation—he creates other individuals and future generations. This is an urge toward survival through children.

Dynamic three is groups; the urge on the part of the individual to survive as part of a group (with the individual himself furnishing this motivation). That covers any kind of a group—temporary or permanent groups, political groups, social groups or anything like this.

Dynamic four is survival through man as a species. Even if you had an American and Russian and they were army officers and highly antagonistic toward each other, and if one of Orson Welles'[3] men from Mars suddenly showed up, you would find these two men joining hands to shoot the devil out of that foreign species, if it were conceived to be a menace to man. Man actually works on the fourth dynamic. War is a breakdown on this dynamic.

Dynamic five pertains to life—just life in general. That is vegetables, fish, trees, any kind of life. On the fifth dynamic an individual survives to make life survive.

---

3. **Orson Welles:** (1915–1985) American actor, director and producer. Produced a radio dramatization in 1938 of H.G. Wells' *The War of the Worlds.* It was done in the form of a news broadcast and caused widespread panic in the US at the time when people thought that the Martians had actually invaded the Earth. *See also* **Wells, H.G.** in the glossary.

The sixth dynamic is the dynamic we call MEST—a term made from the first letter of each of the words *matter, energy, space* and *time*. That is the material universe. The individual actually has a thrust for the survival of the material universe.

The seventh dynamic is the dynamic of the spirit, the urge toward existence as or of spirits.

The eighth dynamic we write as a number eight on its side, which stands for infinity, and this would be the dynamic of a Supreme Being, a Prime Mover Unmoved[4] or Creator.

By inspection of man himself, an individual seems to have a thrust in each one of these departments. In other words, an individual is interested in the survival of groups on a parity[5] with his own survival.

As soon as you knock out one of these dynamics on a human being and you say "For this individual, this dynamic cannot possibly exist," you get trouble, because they *all* get knocked out. They come down on the same level. In other words, if you cut out half of one dynamic, you have cut out half of the rest of the dynamics. This package of dynamics is very vital to the survival of an individual.

Right now we have a whole society which is educated along the line of "man thinks for himself alone." People have to be forced, whipped, beaten and educated to have a third dynamic. They have to be jailed, they

---

4. **Prime Mover Unmoved:** a concept originating with the Greek philosopher Aristotle. It means the first cause of all movement, itself immovable.

5. **parity:** equality, as in amount, status, character.

have to be sent to school, they have to be punished, fined, taxed, made to go to the polls and vote Democratic. All of these various things have to be done in order to make a person have a third dynamic.

In other words, in this society they are working like mad to build something which is already there. But take away all of these big structures of socialization[6] of the individual and you will find lying behind these structures a much prettier structure and a much stauncher one than any artificial structure being built.

It is the same way on the fourth dynamic. Have you ever known anyone who thought only cats were fit to associate with and that man was no good? There are such people, I assure you. "Men are no good. Men are cruel, they're beasts, they do terrible things. And the human race is no good and man is no good. But cats and dogs and dear little dumb animals, these are what are nice." In other words, this person throws it all over on the fifth dynamic. She will be all right and she can go on living only until that concept fails on her, because it is an artificial concept.

Man can do almost anything he wants to these dynamics as long as he is consistent about it. The second he gets inconsistent along any line he is in bad shape.

An optimum solution of life takes into account the maximum survival for everything concerned in the problem. This does not mean that one cannot destroy. It so happens that if we didn't have destruction as one

---

6. **socialization:** the action of training (an individual) for society or a social environment.

of the operating methods of existence, we would be in pretty bad shape. Do you realize that every fern tree that was growing back in the earliest ages would still be growing, and this would be in addition to every tree that had grown since? And we would have live, growing trees on the face of the Earth until we would probably be walking about eight hundred feet above the soil. Death—destruction—has to come in there and clear the way for advances and improvements. And destruction, when used in that way, is very legitimate.

For instance, you can't build an apartment house without knocking down the tenement[7] that stood there before. Somebody comes along and says, "Oh, that's very bad; you're destroying something. You're destroying an old landmark."

"We're trying to put up an apartment house here, lady."

"Yes, but that's a famous old landmark."

"Lady, that thing is about ready to fall into the street."

"Oh, it's very bad to destroy things."

That is pretty aberrated, because you have to destroy something once in a while. Just think what would happen, for instance, if every piece of paper that had ever been given you in your lifetime was still in your possession and then you had to move, and it was very bad to destroy things so you had to keep on lugging

---

7. **tenement:** a rundown and often overcrowded apartment house, especially in a poor section of a large city.

all these things around with you. You can see how ridiculous it would get.

There is an actual equation[8] involved in this: One must not destroy beyond the necessity required in construction. If one starts to destroy beyond the necessity required in construction, one gets into pretty bad shape very hurriedly. One gets into the shape Nazi Germany was in. They destroyed everything; they said, "Now Austria, now Czechoslovakia, now let's knock apart Stalingrad![9]" So they did and Stalingrad was an awful mess. So was Germany.

There is an old truism, "Never send to know for whom the bell tolls; it tolls for thee." Nothing is truer. People start looking at this and they get superstitions about it. They say, "Well, I don't dare harm anybody else because then I would be harmed someplace or other." This is not necessarily true. But on the overall equation of life and existence, the willful destruction of something can upset the survival of the other entities in its vicinity. It can upset and overbalance things to a point of where, for example, we don't have any more passenger pigeons.[10] People didn't stop and think, back there a hundred years ago, that one of these fine days there

---

8. **equation:** a condition involving some equivalence or relation.

9. **Stalingrad:** former name of Volgograd, a city on the Volga River in the country of Russia. Stalingrad was the site of a crucial battle against the invading German army in World War II (Aug. 1942 to Feb. 1943). Although the city was practically destroyed, Russia's defense finally forced the Germans to retreat and then surrender. The battle was the turning point in Germany's military power in the war and is considered one of the great turning points in military history.

10. **passenger pigeons:** long-tailed American pigeons, noted for their extended migratory flights, but extinct since 1914. Passenger pigeons are believed to have lived in greater numbers than any other vertebrate (having a backbone) land animal of which records exist, but were repeatedly slaughtered in the 1800s for US food markets during the height of their breeding season.

wouldn't be any—obviously, there were all kinds of them all over the sky.

So man has had to go into a tremendous game-conservation[11] program in order to restore the wildlife which his grandfathers wiped out. Man will do this quite instinctively.

The dynamics mean, simply, how many forms of survival are there? How does an individual survive? You can work this out that the individual survives solely because of himself and cooperates only because of self-ishness. But you can also work it out that he survives only for future generations and prove it all very beautifully that way. You can work it out, as they have in Russia, that the individual survives solely for the state and is only part of an ant society, a collectivist. And so it goes, one right after the other. You can take these ways he survives and you can make each one *it*. But when you put it to the test, you find out that you need all of the dynamics.

The number of dynamics merely add up to the number of fields or entities a man has to be in cooperation with in order to get along.

The optimum solution to any problem would be that solution which did the maximum construction or creation along the maximum number of dynamics pertinent to the problem.

❀

---

11. **game-conservation:** the official protection and care of wild animals, birds and fish which are hunted or caught for sport or for food.

9 How to Live with Children

9

How to Live
with Children

An adult has certain rights around children which the children and modern adults rather tend to ignore. A good, stable adult with love and tolerance in his heart is about the best therapy a child can have.

The main consideration in raising children is the problem of training them without breaking them. You want to raise your child in such a way that you don't have to control him, so that he will be in full possession of himself at all times. Upon that depends his good behavior, his health, his sanity.

Children are not dogs. They can't be trained like dogs are trained. They are not controllable items. They are, and let's not overlook the point, men and women. A child is not a special species of animal distinct from man. A child is a man or a woman who has not attained full growth.

Any law which applies to the behavior of men and women applies to children.

How would you like to be pulled and hauled and ordered about and restrained from doing whatever you wanted to do? You'd resent it. The only reason a child "doesn't" resent it is because he's small. You'd half murder somebody who treated you, an adult, with the orders, contradiction and disrespect given to the average child. The child doesn't strike back because he isn't big enough. He gets your floor muddy, interrupts your nap, destroys the peace of the home instead. If he had equality with you in the matter of rights, he'd not ask for this "revenge." This "revenge" is standard child behavior.

A child has a right to his self-determinism.[1] You say that if he is not restrained from pulling things down on himself, running into the road, etc., etc., he'll be hurt. What are you, as an adult, doing to make that child live in rooms or an environment where he *can* be hurt? The fault is yours, not his, if he breaks things.

The sweetness and love of a child is preserved only so long as he can exert his own self-determinism. You interrupt that and, to a degree, you interrupt his life.

There are only two reasons why a child's right to decide for himself has to be interrupted—the fragility and danger of his environment and *you*. For you work out on him the things that were done to you, regardless of what you think.

When you give a child something, it's his. It's not still yours. Clothes, toys, quarters, what he has been given *must remain under his exclusive control.* So he tears up his shirt, wrecks his bed, breaks his fire engine. It's *none of your business.* How would you like to have somebody give you a Christmas present and then tell you, day after day thereafter, what you are to do with it, and even punish you if you failed to care for it the way the donor wishes? You'd wreck that donor and ruin that present. You know you would. The child wrecks your nerves when you do it

---

1. **self-determinism:** power of choice; power of decision; ability to decide or determine the course of one's actions.

to him. That's revenge. He cries. He pesters you. He breaks your things. He "accidentally" spills his milk. And he wrecks the possession, *on purpose*, about which he is so often cautioned. Why? Because he is fighting for his own self-determinism, his own right to own and make his weight felt on his environment. This "possession" is another channel by which he can be controlled. So he has to fight the possession and the controller.

In raising your child you must avoid "training" him into a social animal. Your child begins by being more sociable, more dignified than you are. In a relatively short time, the treatment he gets so checks him that he revolts. This revolt can be intensified until he is a terror to have around. He will be noisy, thoughtless, careless of possessions, unclean—anything, in short, which will annoy you. Train him, control him and you'll lose his love. You've lost the child forever that you seek to control and own.

Permit a child to sit on your lap. He'll sit there, contented. Now put your arms around him and constrain him to sit there. Do this, even though he wasn't even trying to leave. Instantly, he'll squirm. He'll fight to get away from you. He'll get angry. He'll cry. Recall now, he was happy before you started to hold him. You should actually make this experiment.

Your efforts to mold, train, control this child in general react on him exactly like trying to hold him on your lap.

Of course, you will have difficulty if this child of yours has already been trained, controlled, ordered about, denied his own possessions. In midflight, you change your tactics. You try to give him his freedom. He's so suspicious of you, he will have a terrible time trying to adjust. The transition period will be terrible. But at the end of it, you'll have a well-ordered, well-trained, social child, thoughtful of you and, very important to you, a child who loves you.

The child who is under constraint, shepherded, handled, controlled, has a very bad anxiety postulated. His parents are survival entities. They mean food, clothing, shelter, affection. This means he wants to be near them. He wants to love them, naturally, being their child.

But on the other hand, his parents are nonsurvival entities. His whole being and life depend upon his rights to use his own decision about his movements and his possessions and his body. Parents seek to interrupt this out of the mistaken idea that a child is an idiot who won't learn unless "controlled." So he has to fight shy,[2] to fight against, to annoy and harass an enemy.

Here is anxiety. "I love them dearly. I also need them. But they mean an interruption of my ability, my mind, my potential life. What am I going to do about my parents? I can't live with them. I can't live without them. Oh, dear, oh, dear!" There he sits in his rompers[3] running this problem through his head. That problem, that anxiety, will be with him for eighteen years, more or less. And it will half wreck his life.

Freedom for the child means freedom for you.

---

2. **fight shy:** keep away from; avoid.
3. **rompers:** a loose outer garment, usually consisting of short bloomers and top, worn by young children at play.

Abandoning the possessions of the child to their fate means eventual safety for the child's possessions.

What terrible willpower is demanded of a parent not to give constant streams of directions to a child!

But it has to be done, if you want a well, a happy, a careful, a beautiful, an intelligent child!

Another thing is the matter of contribution. You have no right to deny your child the right to contribute. A human being feels able and competent only so long as he is permitted to contribute as much as or more than he has contributed to him.

A baby contributes by trying to make you smile. The baby will show off. A little older he will dance for you, bring you sticks, try to repeat your work motions to help you. If you don't accept those smiles, those dances, those sticks, those work motions in the spirit they are given, you have begun to interrupt the child's contribution. Now he will start to get anxious. He will do unthinking and strange things to your possessions in an effort to make them "better" for you. You scold him. That finishes him.

The child has a duty toward you. He has to be able to take care of you, not an illusion that he is, but actually. And you have to have patience to allow yourself to be cared for sloppily until, by sheer experience itself—not by your directions—he learns how to do it well. Care for the child? Nonsense. He has probably got a better grasp of immediate situations than you have.

10 ON MARRIAGE

10

On Marriage

Communication is the root of marital success from which a strong union can grow, and noncommunication is the rock on which the ship will bash out her keel.[1]

In the first place, men and women aren't too careful "on whom they up and marry." In the absence of any basic training about neurosis,[2] psychosis,[3] or how to judge a good cook or a good wage earner, that tricky, treacherous and not always easy-to-identify thing called "love" is the sole guiding factor in the selection of mates. It is too much to expect of a society above the level of ants to be entirely practical about an institution as basically impractical as marriage. Thus, it is not amazing that the misselection of partners goes on with such abandon.

There are ways, however, not only to select a marriage partner, but also to guarantee the continuation of that marriage; and these ways are simple. They depend uniformly upon communication.

There should be some parity of intellect and sanity

---

1. keel: the chief timber or steel piece extending along the entire length of the bottom of a boat or ship and supporting the frame: it sometimes protrudes beneath the hull.
2. neurosis: an emotional state containing conflicts and emotional data inhibiting the abilities or welfare of the individual.
3. psychosis: any severe form of mental disorder; insanity.

between a husband and wife for them to have a successful marriage. In Western culture, it is expected that the women shall have some command of the humanities and sciences. It is easy to establish the educational background of a potential marriage partner; it is not so easy to gauge their capability regarding sex, family or children, or their sanity.

In the past, efforts were made to establish sanity with inkblots,[4] square blocks and tests with marbles to find out if anybody had lost any. The resulting figures had to be personally interpreted with a crystal ball and then reinterpreted for application.

In Scientology, there is a test for sanity and comparative sanity which is so simple that anyone can apply it. What is the "communication lag" of the individual? When asked a question, how long does it take him to answer? When a remark is addressed to him, how long does it take for him to register and return? The fast answer tells of the fast mind and the sane mind, providing the answer is a sequitur;[5] the slow answer tells of downscale.[6] Marital partners who have the same communication lag will get along; where one partner is fast and one is slow, the situation will become unbearable to the fast partner and miserable to the slow one.

The repair of a marriage which is going on the rocks does not always require the processing of the marriage

4. **inkblots:** any of a group of irregular patterns made by blots of ink and used in psychological testing.
5. **sequitur:** *(Latin)* that which follows as a consequence; that which follows logically.
6. **downscale:** down the Tone Scale; into a state of decreased awareness; into the lower-level emotions, such as apathy, anger, etc. *See also* **Tone Scale** in the glossary.

partners. It may be that another family factor is in the scene. This may be in the person of a relative, such as the mother-in-law. How does one solve this factor without using a shotgun? This, again, is simple. The mother-in-law, if there is trouble in the family, is responsible for cutting communication lines or diverting communication. One or the other of the partners, then, is cut off the communication channel on which he belongs. He senses this and objects strenuously to it.

Jealousy is the largest factor in breaking up marriages. Jealousy comes about because of the insecurity of the jealous person, and the jealousy may or may not have foundation. This person is afraid of hidden communication lines and will do anything to try to uncover them. This acts upon the other partner to make him feel that his communication lines are being cut; for he thinks himself entitled to have open communication lines, whereas his marital partner insists that he shut many of them. The resultant rows[7] are violent, as represented by the fact that where jealousy exists in a profession such as acting, insurance companies will not issue policies—the suicide rate is too high.

The subject of marriage could not be covered in many chapters, but here is given the basic clue to a successful marriage—Communicate!

※

---

7. **rows:** noisy quarrels, disputes or disturbances; squabbles, brawls or commotions.

11 THE ANATOMY OF FAILURE

THIS BOOK ANSWERS!

You can search the Encyclopedia Britannica from astronomy to the zodiac and still you won't find the answers you are looking for. That's where this book is different. You ask. It answers. It's called

What Is Scientology?

You've already found truth in SCIENTOLOGY. About living, about you.

Now it's time for the full picture. SCIENTOLOGY is a vast subject and that's why we compiled this book. To show you that there's a gradient approach to complete knowledge of self and spiritual freedom. It'll show you how to get started.

You'll see the scope of SCIENTOLOGY in the world, learn what it means to be a SCIENTOLOGIST™ and what it is that makes SCIENTOLOGY a way of life.

This book answers **all** your questions.

864 pages, hardcover, packed with information, photos, illustrations, graphs and more.

- What the spirit, mind and body are.
- The life of its founder L. Ron Hubbard.
- The background and origins of SCIENTOLOGY.
- Programs for literacy, education, drug rehab, criminal reform, all salvaging a world gone mad.
- SCIENTOLOGY® principles and application.
- What auditing is.
- A complete description of **all** the services in SCIENTOLOGY.
- Stories from those who know and use SCIENTOLOGY every day.
  Get *What Is Scientology?*
  It's your reference for life.

TO ORDER BY PHONE OR FOR MORE INFORMATION, CALL TOLL FREE 1-800-334-5433

(See reverse side for order form)

WHAT IS SCIENTOLOGY?
ORDER FORM

☐ **YES!** Please send me my copy of *What Is Scientology?*

   ☐ Hardback $90.00 (includes shipping and handling)

   ☐ Paperback $24.95 (includes shipping and handling)

Name

Address

City

State

Zip

Phone

   ☐ I have enclosed Check/Money Order

   ☐ Please bill my ☐ MasterCard ☐ VISA

Credit Card Number   Exp. Date

Signature   Total $

Send this card in a stamped envelope to the address below. Your book will be shipped to you within 24 hours of receipt.

Send to: *Bridge Publications, Inc.*
                   4751 Fountain Avenue
                   Los Angeles, CA 90029

11

The Anatomy
of Failure

Two things are of paramount importance in Scientology. They are WIN and LOSE.

A person can be stuck in either wins or loses. This might come as a surprise that a person could be stuck in a win, but the facts of a case are that a person is stuck in any reversal between intention or expectance. One knows of the man who lives forever after his having won the race and one knows as well the man who lives forever after the failure of his business.

Primarily, the person who is living forever after in some sort of incident is living the survival of something which overwhelmed him rather than his own survival.

The anatomy of winning or losing, either one, is the anatomy of postulate and reverse-postulate. One intends to do something by making a postulate that it will take place, yet something else takes place. This is a reversal of postulate.

Now let us consider exactly what a failure is. It is only a failure of postulate. It is the failure of an intention. The intention is one thing, the result of the intention is a reverse. This is a failure.

One would say, offhand, that a person who ran a car into a stone wall would have a failure. However, this is simply a social belief that one should not run cars into the wall. There are four conditions which could be involved with running a car into the wall. Running a car into the wall is not a failure without the addition of postulates.

One does not intend to run the car into the wall and yet runs it into the wall. This is a failure.

One intends to run the car into the wall and runs the car into the wall. This is a win.

One intends not to run the car into the wall and doesn't run it into the wall. This is a win.

One intends to run the car into the wall and doesn't run the car into the wall. This is a failure.

Thus we can see that running the car into the wall, or not running the car into the wall, do not themselves establish, except by public agreement as to the conditions of failure, an actual failure. The failure derives from failing to do what one intended to do. When one does what one intends to do, one has a win. When one intends to do one thing and accomplishes something else, one has a lose.

A person is stuck in "wins" only when he intended to lose, and won. A runner never expected to win. He was simply part of the field most of his career and then spectacularly, and almost by accident, he won. It is certain that he will be stuck in that win. Therefore, the only wins that a person gets stuck in are those which were not intentional.

Regret itself is entirely the study of the reversed postulate. One intended to do something good and one did something bad. Similarly, it could also happen that one intended to do something bad and accidentally did something good. Either incident would be regretted. Examples of the first condition are easy to conceive. In the second category, I once knew a man who intended to "get the best of" a woman of somewhat herculean[1] proportions. Somewhere in this contest the woman fell ill and he healed her and did it to such an excellent degree that the woman, to whom mercy was unknown, thereafter promptly overwhelmed him entirely. Here we have the public belief that to heal is good, but in this particular case it was regretted by the individual and would have been regretted even though he did not experience a later loss.

It is an interesting commentary upon the mental anatomy of man that he seldom intends to do something good without actually accomplishing something good. One can always go upstairs into doing well. Failures are the most marked when one intends to do something bad and doesn't accomplish it. For instance, a gunman misses his enemy. He generally lives to regret it because his intention basically was not for the greatest good for the greatest number of dynamics—the definition of good.

Failure consists exactly of something else happening rather than the intention.

An example of this: We are taught that "All men are nice to everyone, there is no murder or insanity or upset

---

1. **herculean:** having enormous strength, courage or size.

anywhere in life," and so gradually we intend that a smooth, uneventful and fruitful life will result. Then we discover that people do bad things to people, that people nag us so that they impede us. That our goals, ambitions and accomplishments are not worthwhile in other people's opinions, and so we have a failure. Here the failure is actually the failure of having a right intention toward life. What is the right intention toward life? To be very, very safe, it is the intention to have happen what will happen. If one knows that life is going to be tricky, cruel, arduous and vicious at times, then one is not surprised by it. One does not hope so sanguinely,[2] or one does not intend so ferociously that all will be "sweetness and light"[3] and one is not so dismayed when "sweetness and light" does not occur.

Romantic novels teach us that the hero always wins and that good always triumphs. Now, it so happens that the hero doesn't always win and that good does not always triumph. On a shorter view we can see villainy triumphing all about us. The truth of the matter is that the villainy is sooner or later going to lose in an entirely different way than the villain expects. One cannot go through life victimizing one's fellow beings and wind up in anything but a trap—the victim himself. However, one doesn't observe this in the common course of life. One sees the villains succeeding everywhere, evidently amassing money, cutting their brother's throat, receiving the fruits of the courts and coming to rule over men.

---

2. **sanguinely:** in a cheerfully optimistic, hopeful or confident manner.
3. **sweetness and light:** persons or things exhibiting unusual tolerance, understanding or sympathy (often used ironically when such a display is entirely out of character).

Without looking at the final consequence of this, which is there just as certainly as the sun rises and sets, one begins to believe that evil triumphs whereas one has been taught that only good triumphs. This causes the person himself to have a failure and actually causes his downfall. The safe way to intend life to go on happening is the way life goes on happening. A much healthier attitude is to change life where one can change it and not be heartbroken because one has not changed it further. In other words, one can intend to change life for the better and can succeed. With Scientology, particularly, he can accomplish this. Before Scientology he probably couldn't, so it would not have been safe or healthy to expect to change life in any way. But now he can at least change life in the sphere where he exists, and thus that things can become better becomes an actuality.

※

12 ACCEPTANCE LEVEL

12

ACCEPTANCE LEVEL[1]

One thing that a person will discover is that he has been carefully taught that certain things are bad and therefore not enjoyable; and that he has set up resistances to these things and that they, at length— these resistances—have become a sponge for the things they were set up to counteract; and the resistance, caving in,[2] has created a hunger for that which was, at first, resisted.

This is the physical universe at work in its very best operation: Make one fight something, then so arrange it that one winds up craving for what one was fighting.

You can, if you look about you, see acceptance level dramatized[3] in every activity of life. You can understand, then, why some woman will not clean up a living room: A living room is not acceptable except in a cluttered fashion to this person. You can understand, also, why some man leaves a beautiful and helpful girl and runs off with a maid or a prostitute: his acceptance level was too far below the beautiful girl. You can understand, too, some of you, why you were not acceptable in your own homes when you were young: you were too bright and too cheerful and this was too high above those around you. You can understand, as well, why the newspapers print the stories they do.

❧

1. **acceptance level:** the degree of a person's willingness to accept people or things freely, monitored and determined by his consideration of the state or condition that those people or things must be in for him to be able to do so.
2. **caving in:** giving in; yielding; submitting.
3. **dramatized:** acted out; demonstrated.

13 CONFRONTING

13

CONFRONTING

That which a person can confront, he can handle.

The first step of handling anything is gaining an ability to face it.

It could be said that war continues as a threat to man because man cannot confront war. The idea of making war so terrible that no one will be able to fight it is the exact reverse of fact—if one wishes to end war. The invention of the longbow,[1] gunpowder, heavy naval cannon, machine guns, liquid fire[2] and the hydrogen bomb add only more and more certainty that war *will* continue. As each new element which man cannot confront is added to elements he has not been able to confront so far, man engages himself upon a decreasing ability to handle war.

We are looking here at the basic anatomy of all problems. Problems start with an inability to confront anything. Whether we apply this to domestic quarrels or to insects, to garbage dumps or Picasso,[3] one can always trace the beginning of any existing problem to an unwillingness to confront.

---

1. **longbow:** a large bow drawn by hand and shooting a long, feathered arrow.
2. **liquid fire:** flaming petroleum or the like, as employed against an enemy in warfare.
3. **Picasso:** Pablo Picasso (1881–1973), Spanish painter and sculptor. Known as one of the foremost twentieth-century artists.

Let us take a domestic scene. The husband or the wife cannot confront the other, cannot confront second dynamic consequences, cannot confront the economic burdens, and so we have domestic strife. The less any of these actually are confronted, the more problem they will become.

It is a truism that one never solves anything by running away from it. Of course, one might also say that one never solves cannonballs by baring his breast to them. But I assure you that if nobody cared whether cannonballs were fired or not, control of people by threat of cannonballs would cease.

Down on skid row[4] where flotsam and jetsam[5] exist to keep the police busy, we could not find one man whose basic difficulties, whose downfall, could not be traced at once to an inability to confront. A criminal once came to me whose entire right side was paralyzed. Yet, this man made his living by walking up to people in alleys, striking them and robbing them. Why he struck people he could not connect with his paralyzed side and arm. From his infancy he had been educated not to confront men. The nearest he could come to confronting men was to strike them, and so his criminal career.

The more the horribleness of crime is deified by television and public press, the less the society will be able to handle crime. The more formidable is made the juvenile delinquent, the less the society will be able to handle the juvenile delinquent.

---

4. **skid row:** a slum street or section full of cheap saloons, rooming houses, etc., frequented by derelicts (penniless persons who are homeless and jobless).
5. **flotsam and jetsam:** transient, unemployed people.

In education, the more esoteric[6] and difficult a subject is made, the less the student will be able to handle the subject. When a subject is made too formidable by an instructor, the more the student retreats from it. There were, for instance, some early European mental studies which were so complicated and so incomprehensible and which were sown with such lack of understanding of man that no student could possibly confront them.

Man at large today is in this state with regard to the human spirit. For centuries man was educated to believe in demons, ghouls[7] and things that went boomp in the night. There was an organization in southern Europe which capitalized upon this terror and made demons and devils so formidable that at length man could not even face the fact that any of his fellows had souls. And thus we entered an entirely materialistic age. With the background teaching that no one can confront the "invisible," vengeful religions sought to move forward into a foremost place of control. Naturally, it failed to achieve its goal and irreligion[8] became the order of the day, thus opening the door for communism and other idiocies. Although it might seem true that one cannot confront the invisible, who said that a spirit was *always* invisible? Rather, let us say that it is impossible for man or anything else to confront the nonexistent; and thus when nonexistent gods are invented and are given more roles in the society, we discover man becomes so degraded that he cannot even confront the spirit in his fellows, much less become moral.

---

6. **esoteric:** beyond the understanding or knowledge of most people.
7. **ghouls:** *(Oriental folklore)* evil spirits that rob graves and feed on the flesh of the dead.
8. **irreligion:** an indifference or hostility to religion.

Confronting, as a subject in itself, is intensely interesting. Indeed, there is some evidence that mental image pictures[9] occur only when the individual is unable to confront the circumstances of the picture. When this compounds and man is unable to confront anything anywhere, he might be considered to have pictures of everything everywhere. This is proven by a rather interesting test made in 1947 by myself. I discovered, although I did not entirely interpret it at the time, that an individual has no further pictures when he can confront all pictures; thus being able to confront everything he has done, he is no longer troubled with the things he has done. Supporting this, it will be discovered that individuals who progress in an ability to handle pictures eventually have no pictures at all. This we call a Clear.[10]

A Clear, in an absolute sense, would be someone who could confront anything and everything in the past, present and future.

The handling of a problem seems to be simply the increase of ability to confront the problem, and when the problem can be totally confronted, it no longer exists. This is strange and miraculous.

---

9. **mental image pictures:** copies of the physical universe as it goes by; we call a mental image picture a facsimile when it is a "photograph" of the physical universe sometime in the past. We call a mental image picture a mock-up when it is created by the thetan or for the thetan and does not consist of photographs of the physical universe. We call a mental image picture a hallucination, or more properly an automaticity (something uncontrolled), when it is created by another and seen by self.

10. **Clear:** the name of a state achieved through auditing or an individual who has achieved this state. A Clear is a being who no longer has his own reactive mind. A Clear is an unaberrated person and is rational in that he forms the best possible solutions he can on the data he has and from his viewpoint. The Clear has no engrams which can be restimulated to throw out the correctness of computations by entering hidden and false data.

Man's difficulties are a compound of his cowardices. To have difficulties in life, all it is necessary to do is to start running away from the business of livingness.[11] After that, problems of unsolvable magnitude are assured. When individuals are restrained from confronting life, they accrue[12] a vast ability to have difficulties with it.

Various nervous traits can be traced at once to *trying to* confront with something which insists on running away. A nervous hand, for instance, would be a hand with which the individual is trying to confront something. The forward motion of the nervousness would be the effort to make it confront; the backward motion of it would be its refusal to confront. Of course, the basic error is confronting *with* the hand.

The world is never bright to those who cannot confront it. Everything is a dull gray to a defeated army. The whole trick of somebody telling you "it's all bad over there" is contained in the fact that he is trying to keep you from confronting something and thus make you retreat from life. Eyeglasses, nervous twitches, tensions, all of these things stem from an unwillingness to confront. When that willingness is repaired, these disabilities tend to disappear.

❉

---

11. **livingness:** the activity of going along a certain course, impelled (driven) by a purpose and with some place to arrive.
12. **accrue:** accumulate, as by natural growth.

14 ON BRINGING ORDER

14

ON BRINGING ORDER

When you start to introduce order into anything, disorder shows up and blows off.[1] Therefore, efforts to bring order in the society or any part of it will be productive of disorder for a short while every time.

The trick is to keep on bringing order and soon the disorder is gone and you have orderly activity remaining. But if you *hate* disorder and fight disorder only, don't ever try to bring order to anything, for the resulting disorder will drive you half mad.

Only if you can ignore disorder and can understand this principle can you have a working world.

※

---

1. **blows off:** suddenly dissipates (disperses; vanishes).

15 PROFESSIONALISM

15

PROFESSIONALISM

Don't ever do anything as though you were an amateur.

Anything you do, do it as a professional to professional standards.

If you have the idea about *anything* you do that you just dabble in it, you will wind up with a dabble life. There'll be no satisfaction in it because there will be no real production you can be proud of.

Develop the frame of mind that whatever you do, you are doing it as a professional and move up to professional standards in it.

Never let it be said of you that you lived an amateur life.

Professionals *see* situations and they handle what they see. They are not amateur dabblers.

So learn this as a first lesson about life. The only successful beings in any field, including living itself, are those who have a professional viewpoint and make themselves and *are* professionals.

❀

16 ON HUMAN CHARACTER

16

ON HUMAN CHARACTER

In the past, a knowledge of his own character was an unpalatable fact to man, since people sought to force him to achieve that knowledge solely through condemnation. He resisted what he was and he became what he resisted; and ever with a dwindling spiral, he reached lower dregs. If ever once a man were to realize with accuracy what he was, if he were to realize what other people sought to make him, if he could attain this knowledge with great certainty, there are no chains strong enough to prevent his escaping; for such would be his astonishment that he would brave beasts, gods and Lucifer[1] himself to become something better than what he had beheld in his own heart.

The only tragedy of all this is that man has lacked any method of estimating himself with certainty so as to know what it was he was trying to improve.

The basic impulse of man is to produce an effect.

In relatively high-toned beings,[2] the very upper

---

1. **Lucifer:** the chief rebel angel who was cast out of heaven; Satan; the Devil.
2. **high-toned beings:** individuals who are high on the Tone Scale. They think wholly into the future. They are extroverted toward their environment. They clearly observe the environment with full perception unclouded by undistinguished fears about the environment. They think very little about themselves but operate automatically in their own interests. They enjoy existence. Their calculations are swift and accurate. They are very self-confident. They *know* they know and do not even bother to assert that they know. They control their environment.

range of man and above, the impulse is to produce something out of nothing: One can only cause a creative effect by causing nothingnesses to become something.

Lower on the Tone Scale,[3] the effect most desired is to make nothing out of something. The general range of man occupies this area of the scale.

Man on the lower ranges is entirely dedicated to the goals of the body itself. The body, to exist, must make nothing out of something. This, as the simplest illustration, is the goal of eating. It may or may not be necessary to life to eat; it may not even be necessary for the body to eat. In para-Scientology,[4] there is some evidence that the stomach once produced sufficient life energy to motivate the body without any further "food," but the body of man and beasts in general is not equipped so today, and of that we are very certain.

The body's single effort to make something out of nothing is resident in sex, and in this culture at our time, sex is a degraded and nasty thing which must be hidden at best and babies are something not to have,

3. **Tone Scale:** a scale, in Scientology, which shows the emotional tones of a person. These, ranged from the highest to the lowest, are, in part, serenity, enthusiasm (as we proceed downward), conservatism, boredom, antagonism, anger, covert hostility, fear, grief, apathy. An arbitrary numerical value is given to each level on the scale. There are many aspects of the *Tone Scale* and using it makes possible the prediction of human behavior. For further information on the *Tone Scale,* read the book *Self Analysis* by L. Ron Hubbard.
4. **para-Scientology:** a category of data in Scientology which includes all greater or lesser uncertainties and questionable things; things in Scientology of which the common, normal observer cannot be sure with a little study.

but to be prevented. Thus, even sex has been made to parallel the something-into-nothing impulse.

Exactly as the body, by eating, seeks to make nothing out of something, so does the general run[5] of man, in his conversation and interpersonal relationships, seek to make a nothingness out of friendship, acquaintances, himself, art and all other things. He much more readily accepts a statement or a news story which reduces something further toward nothing than he accepts a story which raises from a relative nothing to a higher something. Thus, we find out that scientific achievements for the good of man occupy a very late place in the newspapers and stories of murders and love nests,[6] wars and plagues gain first place.

Man, in his present form, is held on the road to survival by his culture alone. This culture has been policed into action by brute force. The bulk of men are surviving against their own will. They are working against their own desires, and they seek, wherever possible and ever so covertly, to succumb.

The physical universe could be called a love–hate universe, for these two are the most prominently displayed features, and neither one has any great altitude, although many claim that love is all and that love is high on the Tone Scale, which it is not.

---

5. run: the typical, ordinary or average kind.
6. love nests: dwellings of lovers, especially places where illicit (not allowed by law, custom, rule, etc.) lovers live or meet.

To live, man must eat. Every time a man eats, no matter the kindness of his heart or disposition, something must have died or must die, even though it is only cells. To eat, then, one must be able to bring about death. If eating is motivated by death, then digestion would be as good as one is permitted to kill. Digestions are bad in this society. Killing is shunned in a degraded and covert fashion, and man eats only those things which not only have been killed elsewhere and out of his sight, but have as well been certified as dead through scalding cookery. Killing even food is today far above the ability of the majority of our culture.

The characteristics of love could be said to be no-kill, stomach trouble, hunger but can't eat, work, flows,[7] heavy emphasis on affinity, reality and communication and inhibited sex. Hate as a personality could be said to characterize, at least on a thought level, kill, bowel trouble, hungry but eats covertly, no work, hold, pretended affinity, reality and communication and enforced sex. These are two personality classes. Many people are compounded of both.

Thought in man is largely born out of impact and is not free. It is an effort to know before he knows, which is to say, to prevent a future. The phenomenon of going into the past is simply the phenomenon of trying to take the knowledge which one acquired

---

7. **flows:** progresses of energy between two points.

through force and impact, and held after the event, and place it before the event so as to prevent that thing which has already happened. "If I had only known" is a common phrase. This gets bad enough to cause man to want to know before he looks at anything, for in his debased[8] state it is dangerous not only to use force, not only to use emotion, not only to think, but also to perceive things which do. Thus the prevalence of glasses in this society.

The body—and that means, of course, man in this culture—must have a reason for everything. That which has the most reason is the body. A reason is an explanation, the way man interprets it, and he feels he has to explain himself away and to explain every action which he makes. Man believes he must have force but receives force, that he must not perceive or be perceived, that he must kill but must not be killed, that he must not have emotion, that he must be able to wreak[9] destruction without receiving it. He can have no pain; he must shun work and pretend that all work he does has a definite goal. Everything he sees he feels must have been created by something else and that he himself must not create. Everything has a prior creation to his own. All things must be based on earlier things. Thus, he shuns responsibility for whatever he makes and whatever destruction he may create.

This animal has equipped himself with weapons

---

8. **debased:** lowered in value, quality, character, dignity.
9. **wreak:** inflict; cause.

of destruction far superior to his weapons for healing and in this low-toned mockery[10] whines and pleads that he is duplicating saintliness and godliness; yet he knows no meaning of ethics[11] and can follow only morals.[12] He is a meat animal, a thing in the strait-jacket of a police force, made to survive, made to stay in check, made to do his duty and performing most of it without joy and without, poor thing, even actual suffering. He is a meat animal, he is something to be eaten. If he is to be helped, he must learn where he is and find better.

In our current age, cowardice is an accepted social pose,[13] self-abnegation[14] a proper mode of address, hidden indecency a proper method of survival.

It may be that my statement of this does not carry through with an entire conviction. Fortunately, although these data are based on a wide experience with man, particularly in the last few years, as well as during a terrible and cataclysmic[15] war, my statement

---

10. **low-toned mockery:** a little band down very close to death on the Tone Scale. Anything that is in that band is a mockery of anything higher. Some fellow dresses in a very good way and a comedian comes out on the stage, dressed overdone with the same characteristics. That would be a lower-scale mockery of a person dressing well. *See also* **Tone Scale** in the glossary.

11. **ethics:** rationality toward the highest level of survival for the individual, the future race, the group and mankind. Ethics is reason and the contemplation of optimum survival.

12. **morals:** a code of good conduct laid down out of the experience of the race to serve as a uniform yardstick for the conduct of individuals and groups.

13. **pose:** attitude or frame of mind.

14. **self-abnegation:** lack of consideration for oneself or one's own interest; self-denial.

15. **cataclysmic:** characterized by violent changes; calamities.

of the case does not have to stand, for in Scientology we have the processes which signify the accuracy of this observation on human character.

17 PAST, PRESENT AND FUTURE

17

PAST, PRESENT AND FUTURE

There is a basic rule that a psychotic[1] person is concerned with the past, a neurotic[2] person is barely able to keep up with the present and a sane person is concerned with the future.

This division could be more specifically made by realizing that the neurotic is barely able to confront the present, but that the very, very sane confront the present entirely and have very little concern for the future, being competent enough in handling the present to let the future take care of itself. Looking into the past and looking into the extreme future, alike, are efforts to avoid present time and efforts to look elsewhere than *at* something.

You have known people who would reply on an entirely different subject when asked about anything; when consulted concerning the weather, they would reply about a meteorologist.[3] The inability to look *at* something becomes first manifest by thinking before looking, and then the actual target at which one should be looking is more and more avoided until it is hidden entirely in a mix-up of complications.

---

1. **psychotic:** characterizing a person who is physically or mentally harmful to those about him out of proportion to the amount of use he is to them.
2. **neurotic:** characterizing one who is insane or disturbed on some subject (as opposed to a psychotic person, who is just insane in general).
3. **meteorologist:** a person who studies meteorology, the science dealing with the atmosphere and its phenomena, including weather and climate.

The avoidance of reality is merely an avoidance of present time.

An individual who will not look at the physical universe must look either ahead of it into the future, or behind it into the past. One of the reasons he does this is because there is insufficient action in the present to begin with; and then this thirst for action develops into an inability to have action, and he decides that all must be maintained in a constant state, and he seeks to prevent action. This also applies to pain. People who are somewhat out of present time have a horrible dread of pain; and people who are truly out of present time—as in a psychotic state—have a revulsion towards pain which could not be described. A person entirely within present time is not much concerned with pain.

The avoidance of work is one of the best indicators of a decayed state on the part of a personality. There are two common denominators to all aberrated personalities: One of these is a horror of work and the other is a horror of pain. People only mildly out of present time, which is to say, people who are categorized as "sane," have already started to apologize about work, in that they work toward an end reward and no longer consider that the output of effort itself and the accomplishment of things is sufficient reward in itself. Thus, the whole network[4] of gratitude or admiration as necessary pay for energy put forth. The parental demand for gratitude is often reflected in a severely aberrated person who is given to feel he can never repay the enormous favors conferred on him by

---

4. **network:** any system of lines or channels interlacing or crossing like the fabric of a net; also used figuratively, as, for example, a network of falsehoods.

being worked for by his parents. Actually, they need not to be paid; for, flatly, if it was not sufficient reward to do the work of raising him, they are beyond being paid; in other words, they could not accept pay.

Taking the very, very sane person in present time, one would mark a decline of his sanity by a shift from an interest in present time to an overwhelming interest in the future which would decline into considerable planning for the future in order to avoid bad things happening in it; to, finally, a shunning of the future because of painful incidents; to a shuddering and tenuous[5] hold on present time; and, then, an avoidance of both the future and present time and a shift into the past. This last would be a psychotic state.

One holds onto things in the past on the postulate that they must not happen in the future. This sticks the person in the past.

Inaction and indecision in the present is because of fear of consequences of the future. In Scientology this condition in an individual can be remedied so that he can more comfortably face present time.

✻

---

5. tenuous: weak; flimsy.

18 PLAYING THE GAME

18

PLAYING THE GAME[1]

The highest activity is playing a game. When one is high-toned, he knows that it is a game. As he falls away down the Tone Scale, he becomes less and less aware of the game.

The greatest ability of thought is *differentiation*.[2] So long as one can differentiate, one is sane. Its opposite is *identification*.[3]

The legal definition of sanity is the "ability to tell right from wrong."

Therefore, the highest ability in playing a game would be the ability to know the rightness and wrongness rules of that particular game. As all rightness and wrongness are considerations, and as the game itself is a consideration, the playing of the game requires a high ability to differentiate; particularly, it requires an ability to know the rules and the right rules and the wrong rules.

When an individual is prone to identify, he is no

---

1. **game:** a contest of person against person or team against team. A game consists of freedom, barriers and purposes. It also consists of control and uncontrol. An opponent in a game must be an uncontrolled factor, otherwise one would know exactly where the game was going and how it would end and it would not be a game at all.
2. **differentiation:** the ability to "tell the difference" between one person and another, one object and another. It indicates a person is sane. As soon as he begins to confuse his wife with his mother or his coat with his father's coat, he is on the road toward insanity.
3. **identification:** the inability to evaluate differences in time, location, form, composition or importance.

longer able to differentiate the right rules and the wrong rules, and the right rules become wrong and the wrong rules become right, and we have a criminal.

A criminal cannot play the game of society. He plays, then, the "game" called "cops and robbers."

A person who strongly identifies is not necessarily a criminal, but he certainly is having trouble playing the game of society. Instead of playing that game, he "gets tired," "gets sick." He has these things happen because he doesn't want to play the social game. He has a "game" of sorts in "hypochondria."[4]

Now, if you had a culture which was running a no-game game for anybody, a culture which itself had no game for everybody to play, a culture which had in its government a fixation on keeping anyone from playing the game *they* wanted to play, we would have, as its manifestation, all manner of curious ills, such as those described in various ideologies like capitalism or communism. The entire government game would be "Stop playing *your* game." The degree of sanity in government would be the degree it permitted strong and active participation in the game of government, in the game of playing your game.

But, if people who can't play the game can't differentiate, similarly, a sane person could find himself very confused to be part of a game which wasn't differentiating and where the rightness and wrongness rules

---

4. **hypochondria:** *(psychiatry)* an excessive preoccupation with one's health, usually focused on some particular symptom.

were unclearly defined. Thus, a government without exact and accurate codes and jurisprudence[5] would discover in its citizens an inability to play the game no matter how sane they were.

Thus, the game can be crazy and its players sane or the players can be crazy and the game sane. Either condition would affect the other. When we get crazy players and a crazy game, the end product of either of the two imbalances above, we would get anything except a game. We would get chaos.

As a useful example of an inability to differentiate, let us take people who cannot see anything wrong with slanderous materials. We have here people who see no difference. They don't differentiate. They don't differentiate because they see no game. They see no game because they can't play a game. Or, habituated[6] to a social structure which had no rules of rightness or wrongness, they have lost their criteria.[7]

*

---

5. **jurisprudence:** a system or body of law; a legal system.
6. **habituated:** made used to; accustomed; familiarized with.
7. **criteria:** standards, rules or tests by which things can be judged.

19 THE VOCABULARIES OF SCIENCE

19

THE VOCABULARIES OF SCIENCE

In all scientific systems you have a number of code words which operate as communication carriers, and when a person does not know these words well, he is having difficulty with the science itself. I have seen a senior in science falling down in his comprehension of a later part of the science because he had never gotten the nomenclature[1] of the science straight to begin with. He did not know exactly what a British thermal unit[2] was, or something like that. Therefore, later on, when he's solving some vast and involved problem, there's a datum rambling around in his head and it's not stable at all. It's getting confused. It's mixed up with all other data. And that is only because he didn't understand what the *term* was in the first place.

So, just as you learn semaphore[3] signals, just as you learn Morse code,[4] just as you learn baby talk, so, when you become conversant with any particular specialized subject, you must become conversant with its terminology. Your understanding of it then increases. Otherwise,

---

1. **nomenclature:** the set of terms used to describe things in a particular subject.
2. **British thermal unit:** the quantity of heat required to raise the temperature of one pound of water one degree Fahrenheit.
3. **semaphore:** a system of signaling by the use of two flags, one held in each hand: the letters of the alphabet are represented by the various positions of the arms.
4. **Morse code:** a system by which letters, numbers, punctuation and other signs are expressed by dots, dashes and spaces or by wigwags of a flag, long and short sounds or flashes of light. Morse code is now used mainly in signaling and in some telegraphy.

understanding is impeded by these words rattling around and not joining themselves to anything. If you know vaguely that such and such a word exists and yet have no definite understanding of what it means, it does not align. Thus, a misunderstanding of a word can cause a misalignment of a subject, and this really is the basis of the primary confusion in man's understanding of the mind.

There have been so many words assigned to various parts of the mind that one would be staggered if he merely catalogued all of these things. Take, for instance, the tremendous background and technology of psychoanalysis.[5] Overpoweringly complicated material, most of it is merely descriptive; some of it action terminology, such as the censor,[6] the id,[7] the ego,[8] the alter ego,[9] and whatnot. Most of these things lined up, each one meant a specific thing. But the practitioners who began to study this science did not have a good founding in the exact sciences—in other words, they didn't have a

---

5. **psychoanalysis:** a system of mental therapy developed in 1894 by Sigmund Freud. It depended upon the following practices for its effects: The patient was made to talk about and recall his childhood for years while the practitioner brought about a transfer of the patient's personality to his own and searched for hidden sexual incidents believed by Freud to be the only cause of aberration. The practitioner read sexual significances into all statements and evaluated them for the patient along sexual lines. Each of these points later proved to be based upon false premises and incomplete research, accounting for their lack of result and the subsequent failure of the subject and its offshoots. *See also* **Freud** in the glossary.

6. **censor:** *(psychoanalysis)* in early Freudian dream therapy this was considered to be the force which repressed ideas, impulses and feelings and prevented them from entering consciousness in their original, undisguised forms.

7. **id:** *(psychoanalysis)* the division of the psyche (soul) associated with instinctual impulses and demands for immediate satisfaction of primitive needs.

8. **ego:** *(psychoanalysis)* that part of the psyche (soul) which experiences the external world through the senses, organizes the thought processes rationally and governs action.

9. **alter ego:** *(psychoanalysis)* another aspect of oneself.

model of the exact sciences. And in the humanities, they could be as careless as they liked with their words, because the humanities were not expected to be precise or exact—not a criticism of them, it just means that you could have a lesser command of the language.

When they got into the study of Freud,[10] they got into this interesting thing—to one person an id was one thing and to another person it was something else. And alter ego was this and it was that. The confusion of terms there, practically all by itself, became the totality of confusion of psychoanalysis.

Actually, psychoanalysis is as easy to understand, certainly, as Japanese. Japanese is a baby talk—very, very hard to read, very, very easy to talk. If you can imagine a language which tells you which is the subject, which is the verb, which is the object, every time it speaks, you can imagine this baby-talk kind of a language. One that doesn't have various classes or conjugations[11] of verbs. A very faint kind of a language. Nevertheless, it merely consists, in order to communicate with a Japanese, of knowing the meanings of certain words, and if you know the meanings of those words precisely, then when a Japanese comes up to you and says, "Do you want a cup of tea?" you don't immediately get up because you thought he said "Wet paint." You have a communication possibility.

Well, similarly, with the language of psychoanalysis, the great difficulties inherent in understanding such a

---

10. **Freud:** Sigmund Freud (1856–1939), Austrian physician and the founder of psychoanalysis. *See also* **psychoanalysis** in the glossary.
11. **conjugations:** systematic arrangements of the forms of a verb.

thing as psychoanalysis became much less difficult when one viewed psychoanalysis as a code system to relay certain meanings. It did not, then, become a problem of whether or not these phenomena existed or didn't exist. It simply became a problem of words meaning a certain precise thing. And if they meant that thing to everybody, then everybody was talking psychoanalysis, and if it didn't mean this thing to everybody, then people weren't talking psychoanalysis. Who knows *what* they were talking. The next thing you know, they were talking Jungianism,[12] the next thing you know, they were talking Adlerianism,[13] and the amount of difference between these various items is minute, to say the least. But the language difficulties, then, made many practitioners in that field at odds with the theory, which they did not, at any rate, understand.

I remember one time learning Igoroti, an Eastern primitive language, in a single night. I sat up by kerosene lantern and took a list of words that had been made by an old missionary in the hills in Luzon[14]—the Igorot had a very simple language. This missionary had phoneticized[15] their language and he had made a list of their main words and their usage and grammar. And I remember sitting up under a mosquito net with the mosquitoes hungrily chomping their beaks just outside the net, and

---

12. **Jungianism:** referring to the theories of Carl Gustav Jung (1875–1961), Swiss psychologist and psychiatrist. These include in part a theory of the unconscious and the theory of two attitude types (extroversion and introversion).

13. **Adlerianism:** referring to the theory of Alfred Adler (1870–1937), an Austrian psychiatrist and psychologist. This theory stated in part that behavior is determined by compensation for feelings of inferiority.

14. **Luzon:** main island of the Philippines.

15. **phoneticized:** represented or spelled as they would sound when spoken, using symbols to show pronunciation.

learning this language—three hundred words—just memorizing these words and what they meant. And the next day I started to get them in line and align them with people, and was speaking Igoroti in a very short time.

The point here is that it is not difficult to learn a language if you understand that you are learning a language.

※

20 How to Study a Science

20

How to Study
a Science

The whole subject of a science, as far as the student is concerned, is as good or bad in direct ratio to his knowledge of it. It is up to a student to find out how precise the tools are. He should, before he starts to discuss, criticize or attempt to improve on the data presented to him, find out for himself whether or not the mechanics of a science are as stated and whether or not it does what has been proposed for it.

He should make up his mind about each thing that is taught in the school—the procedure, techniques, mechanics and theory. He should ask himself these questions: Does this piece of data exist? Is it true? Does it work? Will it produce the best possible results in the shortest time?

There are two ways man ordinarily accepts things, neither of them very good. One is to accept a statement because authority says it is true and must be accepted, and the other is by preponderance[1] of agreement amongst other people.

Preponderance of agreement is all too often the general public test for sanity or insanity. Suppose someone were to walk into a crowded room and suddenly point to a ceiling saying, "Oh, look! There's a huge, twelve-foot spider on the ceiling!" Everyone would look

1. preponderance: superiority in weight, power, influence, numbers, etc.

up, but no one else would see the spider. Finally someone would tell him so. "Oh, yes, there is," he would declare, and become very angry when he found that no one would agree with him. If he continued to declare his belief in the existence of the spider, he would very soon find himself institutionalized.

The basic definition of sanity, in this somewhat nebulously learned society, is whether or not a person agrees with everyone else. It is a very sloppy manner of accepting evidence, but all too often it is the primary measuring stick.

And then the rule of authority: "Does Dr. J. Doe agree with your proposition? No? Then, of course, it cannot be true. Dr. Doe is an eminent authority in the field."

A man by the name of Galen[2] at one time dominated the field of medicine. Another man by the name of Harvey[3] upset Galen's cozy position with a new theory of blood circulation. Galen had been agreeing with the people of his day concerning the "tides" of the blood. They knew nothing about heart action. They accepted everything they had been taught and did little observing of their own. Harvey worked at the Royal Medical Academy and found by animal vivisection[4] the actual function of the heart.

---

2. **Galen:** (c. A.D. 130–200) Greek physician. A prolific writer, his works were for centuries the standards for anatomy and physiology.

3. **Harvey:** William Harvey (1578–1657), English physician and discoverer of the mechanics of blood circulation.

4. **vivisection:** medical research consisting of surgical operations or other experiments performed on living animals to study the structure and function of living organs and parts, and to investigate the effects of diseases and therapy.

He had the good sense to keep his findings absolutely quiet for a while. Leonardo da Vinci[5] had somehow discovered or postulated the same thing, but he was a "crazy artist" and no one would believe an artist. Harvey was a member of the audience of a play by Shakespeare[6] in which the playwright made the same observation, but again the feeling that artists never contribute anything to society blocked anyone but Harvey from considering the statement as anything more than fiction.

Finally, Harvey made his announcement. Immediately dead cats, rotten fruit and pieces of wine jugs were hurled in his direction. He raised quite a commotion in medical and social circles until finally, in desperation, one doctor made the historical statement that "I would rather err with Galen than be right with Harvey!"

Man would have made an advance of exactly zero if this had always been the only method of testing evidence. But every so often during man's progress, there have been rebels who were not satisfied with preponderance of opinion, and who tested a fact for themselves, observing and accepting the data of their observation, and then testing again.

Possibly the first man who made a flint axe looked over a piece of flint and decided that the irregular stone could be chipped a certain way. When he found that flint

---

5. **Leonardo da Vinci:** (1452–1519) Italian painter, sculptor, architect, engineer and scientist.
6. **Shakespeare:** William Shakespeare (1564–1616), English poet and dramatist of the Elizabethan period (1558–1603), the most widely known author in all English literature.

would chip easily, he must have rushed to his tribe and enthusiastically tried to teach his fellow tribesmen how to make axes in the shape they desired, instead of spending months searching for accidental pieces of stone of just the right shape. The chances are, he was stoned out of camp.

Indulging in a further flight[7] of fancy,[8] it is not difficult to imagine that he finally managed to convince another fellow that his technique worked, and that the two of them tied down a third with a piece of vine and forced him to watch them chip a flint axe from a rough stone. Finally, after convincing fifteen or twenty tribesmen by forceful demonstration, the followers of the new technique declared war on the rest of the tribe and, winning, forced the tribe to agree by decree.

EVALUATION OF DATA

Man has never known very much about that with which his mind is chiefly filled: data. What is data? What is the evaluation of data?

All these years in which psychoanalysis has taught its tenets[9] to each generation of doctors, the authoritarian method was used; as can be verified by reading a few of the books on the subject. Within them is found, interminably,[10] "Freud said . . ." The truly important thing is not that "Freud said" a thing, but "Is the data valuable? If it is valuable, how valuable is it?" You might

---

7. **flight:** *(figurative)* the act or fact of soaring above or beyond what is ordinary.
8. **fancy:** the power to imagine; imagination.
9. **tenets:** principles, doctrines or beliefs held as truths, as by some group.
10. **interminably:** without, or apparently without, end; endlessly.

say that a datum is as valuable as it has been evaluated. A datum can be proved in ratio to whether it can be evaluated by other data, and its magnitude is established by how many other data it clarifies. Thus, the biggest datum possible would be one which would clarify and identify all knowledge known to man in the material universe.

Unfortunately, however, there is no such thing as a prime[11] datum. There must be not one datum but two data, since a datum is of no use unless it can be evaluated. Furthermore, there must be a datum of similar magnitude with which to evaluate any given datum.

Data is your data only so long as you have evaluated it. It is your data by authority or it is your data. If it is your data by authority, somebody has forced it upon you, and, at best, it is little more than a light aberration. Of course, if you asked a question of a man whom you thought knew his business and he gave you his answer, that datum was not forced upon you. But if you went away from him believing from then on that such a datum existed without taking the trouble to investigate the answer for yourself—without comparing it to the known universe—you were falling short of completing the cycle of learning.

Mechanically, the major thing wrong with the mind is, of course, the turbulence in it; but the overburden of information in this society is enforced education that the individual has never been permitted to test.

---

11. **prime:** primary, original, fundamental; from which others are derived or on which they depend.

Literally, when you are told not to take anyone's word as an absolute datum, you are being asked to break a habit pattern forced upon you when you were a child.

Test it for yourself and convince yourself whether or not it exists as truth. And if you find that it does exist, you will be comfortable thereafter; otherwise, unrecognized even by yourself, you are likely to find, down at the bottom of your information and education, an unresolved question which will itself undermine your ability to assimilate or practice anything in the line of a technique. Your mind will not be as facile[12] on the subject as it should be.

A Look at the Sciences

The reason engineering[13] and physics[14] have reached out so far in advance of other sciences is the fact that they pose problems which punish man so violently if he doesn't look carefully into the physical universe.

An engineer is faced with the problem of drilling a tunnel through a mountain for a railroad. Tracks are laid up to the mountain on either side. If he judges space wrongly, the two tunnel entrances would fail to meet on the same level in the center. It would be so evident to one and all concerned that the engineer made a mistake, that he takes great care not to make such a mistake. He

---

12. **facile:** able to move, act, work, proceed, etc., with ease.
13. **engineering:** the science concerned with putting scientific knowledge to practical uses, divided into different branches, as civil, electrical, mechanical or chemical engineering.
14. **physics:** the science which deals with relationships between matter and energy, including subjects such as mechanics, heat, light, sound, magnetism, radiation and atomic structure.

observes the physical universe, not only to the extent that the tunnel must meet to a fraction of an inch, but to the extent that, if he were to judge wrongly the character of the rock through which he drills, the tunnel would cave in—an incident which would be considered a very unlucky and unfortunate occurrence to railroading.

Biology comes closer to being a science than some others because, in the field of biology, if someone makes too big a mistake about a bug, the immediate result can be dramatic and terrifying. Suppose a biologist is charged with the responsibility of injecting plankton into a water reservoir. Plankton are microscopic "germs" that are very useful to man. But, if through some mistake, the biologist injects typhoid[15] germs into the water supply—there would be an immediate and dramatic result.

Suppose a biologist is presented with the task of producing a culture[16] of yeast[17] which would, when placed in white bread dough, stain the bread brown. This man is up against the necessity of creating a yeast which not only behaves as yeast, but makes a dye as well. He has to deal with the practical aspect of the problem, because after he announces his success, there is the yeast test: Is the bread edible? And the brown-bread test: Is the bread brown? Anyone could easily

---

15. **typhoid:** an infectious, often fatal, febrile (feverish) disease characterized by intestinal inflammation and ulceration, caused by the typhoid bacillus, which is usually introduced with food or drink.

16. **culture:** a growth of bacteria or other microorganisms in a specially prepared nourishing substance.

17. **yeast:** the substance that causes dough for most kinds of bread to rise and that causes beer to ferment. Yeast consists of very small, single-celled plants that grow quickly in a liquid containing sugar.

make the test, and everyone would know very quickly whether or not the biologist had succeeded or failed.

Politics is called a science. There are natural laws about politics. They could be worked out if someone were to actually apply a scientific basis to political research.

For instance, it is a foregone conclusion[18] that if all communication lines are cut between the United States and Russia, Russia and the United States are going to understand each other less and less. Then, by demonstrating to everyone how the American way of life and the Russian way of life are different, and by demonstrating it day after day, year after year, there is no alternative but a break of affinity. By stating flatly that Russia and the United States are not in agreement on any slightest political theory or conduct of man or nations, the job is practically complete. Both nations will go into anger tone and suddenly, there is war.

The United States is a nation possessed of the greatest communications networks on the face of the Earth, with an undreamed-of manufacturing potential. It has within its borders the best advertising men in the world. But instead of selling Europe an idea, it gives machine guns, planes and tanks for use in case Russia breaks out. The more threats imposed against a country in Russia's tone level, the more dangerous that country will become. When people are asked what they would do about this grave question, they shrug and say something to the effect that "the politicians know best." They hedge and

18. **foregone conclusion:** a safe assumption about some future event.

rationalize[19] by saying that, after all, there is the American way of life, and it must be protected.

What is the American way of life? This is a question that will stop almost any American. What is the American way of life that is different from the human way of life? It has tried to gather together economic freedom for the individual, freedom of the press and individual freedom, and define them as a strictly American way of life—why hasn't it been called the human way of life?

In the field of humanities, science has been thoroughly adrift. Unquestioned authoritarian principles have been followed. Any person who accepts knowledge without questioning it and evaluating it for himself is demonstrating himself to be in apathy[20] toward that sphere of knowledge. It demonstrates that the people in the United States today must be in a low state of apathy with regard to politics, in order to accept without question everything that happens.

FUNDAMENTALS

When a man tries to erect the plans of a lifetime or a profession on data which he, himself, has never evaluated, he cannot possibly succeed.

Fundamentals are very, very important, but first of all one must learn how to think in order to be absolutely sure of a fundamental. Thinking is not particularly hard to

---

19. **rationalize:** justify; make excuses to explain irrational behavior.
20. **apathy:** a complete withdrawal from person or people. There is no real attempt to contact oneself and no attempt to contact others. A very docile and obedient, if sick, state of not-beingness. It is near death or an imitation of death. For example, a person in apathy would say, "What's the use? All is lost."

learn. It consists merely of comparing a particular datum with the physical universe as it is known and observed.

Authoritarianism is little more than a form of hypnotism. Learning is forced under threat of some form of punishment. A student is stuffed with data which has not been individually evaluated, just as a taxidermist[21] would stuff a snake. Such a student will be well informed and well educated according to present-day standards, but, unfortunately, he will not be very successful in his chosen profession.

Do not make the mistake of criticizing something on the basis of whether or not it concurs with the opinions of someone else. The point which is pertinent is whether or not it concurs with your opinion. Does it agree with what you think?

Nearly everyone has done some manner of observing of the material universe. No one has seen all there is to see about an organism, for example, but there is certainly no dearth[22] of organisms available for further study. There is no valid reason for accepting the opinion of Professor Blotz of the Blitz University, who said in 1933 that schizophrenics[23] were schizophrenics, and that made them schizophrenics for all time.

If you are interested in the manifestation of insanity, there is any and every form of insanity that you could

---

21. **taxidermist:** one who practices the art of preparing, stuffing and mounting the skins of animals, especially so as to make them appear lifelike.
22. **dearth:** scarcity or lack.
23. **schizophrenics:** persons suffering from schizophrenia, a mental illness in which an individual is being two people madly inside of himself. It is a psychiatry classification derived from the Latin *schizo*, meaning "split," and the Greek *phren*, meaning "mind."

hope to see in a lifetime in almost any part of the world. Study the peculiarities of the people around you and wonder what they would be like if their little peculiarities were magnified a hundredfold. You may find that by listing all the observable peculiarities you would have a complete list of all the insanities in the world. This list might well be far more accurate than that which was advanced by Kraepelin[24] and used in the United States today.

If sanity is rationality and insanity is irrationality, and you postulated how irrational people would be if certain of their obsessions were magnified a hundredfold, you might well have in your possession a far more accurate and complete list of insanities and their manifestations than is currently in existence.

So, the only advice I can give to the student is to study a subject for itself and use it exactly as stated, then form his own opinions. Study it with the purpose in mind of arriving at his own conclusions as to whether or not the tenets he has assimilated are correct and workable. Compare what you have learned with the known universe. Seek for the reasons behind a manifestation, and postulate the manner and in which direction the manifestation will likely proceed. Do not allow the authority of any one person or school of thought to create a foregone conclusion within your sphere of knowledge. Only with these principles of education in mind can you become a truly educated individual.

🐝

---

24. **Kraepelin:** Emil Kraepelin (1856–1926), German psychiatrist. Developed a system of psychiatric classification.

21 RECORDS OF THE MIND ARE PERMANENT

21

RECORDS
OF THE MIND
ARE PERMANENT

Man, for all his years, took the observation for the fact that when a human being was no longer able to control its own operations and functions and so long as it, again in control, could not recall what had occurred, that the material was not recorded. This was wholly unwarranted as an assumption.

Let us examine, first, pain. Pain, technically, is caused by an effort counter to the effort of the individual as a whole.

The individual is a colonial[1] aggregation[2] of cells. Each cell is seeking to live. Each cell and the whole organism is basically motivated by a desire to survive.

The entire physical structure is composed of atoms and molecules, organic[3] and inorganic.[4] While the individual is alive and conscious, these atoms and molecules are in a state of optimum or near optimum tension and alignment.

---

1. **colonial:** of or pertaining to a group of the same kind (of animals, plants or one-celled organisms) living or growing together.
2. **aggregation:** the collecting of separate things into one mass or whole.
3. **organic:** *(chemistry)* of or having to do with compounds containing carbon.
4. **inorganic:** not containing organic matter. Chemical compounds without hydrocarbons (hydrogen and carbon) are usually inorganic.

On the receipt of a counter-effort,[5] such as that of a blow (or, internally, as in the case of drugs, shock or bacteria), the optimum or near optimum tension and alignment of these atoms and molecules, as contained in the nerves, muscles, bones and tissues of the body, are disarranged. The result is a slackening or speeding of the motions of the physical body in such a way as to cause misalignment and maltension[6] of the atoms and molecules.

This is pain. Counter-efforts to survival cause this effect to take place. The technical name of this effect is *randomity*.[7] The directions of motion of the various portions of the body are disarranged into random vectors[8] or patterns. Pain results in loss, invariably—the loss of cells or the loss of general alignment.

When pain departs, it is still on record. The record of that pain can be called again into existence.

If you wish to make a very simple test, simply go back to the last time you hurt yourself. Get as full perceptions as you can of the object which hurt you and the surrounding environment. Seek to contact the

5. **counter-effort:** effort is divided into the effort of the individual himself and the efforts of the environment (physical) against the individual. The individual's own effort is simply called effort. The efforts of the environment are called counter-efforts.

6. **maltension:** *mal-* is a prefix meaning "bad or badly, wrong, ill." *Tension* means "a balancing of forces or elements in opposition." Therefore, *maltension* is bad or wrong balance of forces.

7. **randomity:** a consideration of motion. There is plus randomity and minus randomity. There can be, from the individual's consideration, too much or too little motion, or enough motion. "Enough motion" is measured by the consideration of the individual.

8. **vectors:** physical quantities with both magnitude and direction, such as a force or velocity.

painful object again. Unless you are badly occluded, you should be able to feel that pain once more. If you, yourself, cannot make this test because you are occluded, ask your friends to try it. Sooner or later you will find someone who can recall pain.

Another test: Pinch yourself and then go back to the moment you did it and feel the pinch again. Even if you are occluded, you should be able to do this.

In short, pain is stored on record. But that is not all that is stored. The whole area of any randomity is stored in full. The atoms and molecules rearrange themselves, when pain is recontacted, into the pattern they had when that pain was received. Hence, the pain can come back. But also the effort and all of its perceptions can come back when either the pain or the general randomity come back.

The misalignment caused by a blow, shock, drugs or bacteria causes an inability of the control center of the mind to function. Thus, the control center of the mind can go unconscious, can be overwhelmed by this misalignment.

After consciousness is regained, whenever the control center of the mind tries to recall what happened, it can recall only the randomity. It is trying to recall a time when it could not recall and, thus, draws a blank.

Man thought that if he could not recall a thing, then it didn't record. This is like the little child who hides his eyes and then thinks you can't see him just because he can't see you.

With every area of randomity thus created by injury or illness or shock or drugs, there is stored, as well, the counter-effort to the body. The effort impinged upon the body by the blow or the other misaligning factor also was stored. This is physical force. When it comes back upon the body, it comes back as physical force. It can distort features or the body by being in constant "restimulation."[9]

Restimulation is occasioned by some part of the early recording being approximated in the environment in the present. This calls up the old area of randomity. The body, confused, registers the old counter-effort.

Nearly everyone has these counter-efforts of the past being, some of them, exerted against him in the present. His sublevel awareness is tied up in resisting old counter-efforts—blows, sicknesses, drugs—which once affected him and drove him into unconsciousness.

The moment an individual wholly concentrates his attention elsewhere, these old areas may exert their force again.

Feel the aliveness or full sense of being of each one of the following. Feel wholly alive only in the member of your body named:

1. the right foot

2. the left foot

---

9. **restimulation:** reactivation of a past memory due to similar circumstances in the present approximating circumstances of the past.

3. the right cheek

4. the left cheek

5. the toes

6. the back of the head

7. the back of the neck

8. the nose

9. the right hand

10. the tongue

11. the left hand

12. the stomach

If you have gone over these members, investing carefully aliveness only in each, you probably will have received various aches and pains in areas where your concentration was not fixed, or, at least, experienced grogginess. Try it several times.

Processing cleans up these old areas with resultant rise in health and sanity.

※

22 THE RACE AGAINST MAN'S SAVAGE INSTINCTS

22

THE RACE AGAINST
MAN'S SAVAGE INSTINCTS

For fifty thousand years man has been faced with the enigma of himself and his fellows. Man has been victimized by brutal instincts and impulses which have caused him to erect, in self-protection, prisons, legal codes and complex social systems. Man has not felt safe from man, and indeed, the conduct of man down the ages has not much justified belief or faith: wars, murder, arson, treachery and betrayals, cynicism and destruction have marred his progress, until history itself is a long montage[1] of battles, murders and running blood.

When you teach a child history, what are you teaching him? You are teaching him how this town killed that town, how this king was murdered by that woman, how this war changed the boundaries here and there. It is a pretty strange picture for a civilized being. Not even the apes are indulging in this sort of thing.

Confronted with this aspect in himself and his fellows, man has long searched for an answer to the riddle of his own behavior, for ways to remedy that behavior. Long before Diogenes,[2] man was searching for such

---

1. **montage:** any combination of disparate (different in kind) elements that forms or is felt to form a unified, whole, single image, etc.
2. **Diogenes:** (412?–323 B.C.) Greek philosopher. According to tradition, he once went through the streets holding up a lantern, "looking for an honest man."

answers to his questions. In Babylon,[3] Chaldea,[4] India, and even in the distant primitive times, those men who could think found concern in the antisocial and unreasonable conduct of their fellows.

Man's search for the answer to his own riddle was quickened during the last century by two things: the first was the energy and curiosity of Sigmund Freud, and the second was the mathematics of James Clerk Maxwell[5] and his studies of energy in the physical universe. These two things came up almost simultaneously.

Freud worked without knowledge of the physical universe, which was developed in the years which followed his initial efforts. Freud was not a physical scientist. If anything, he was a mystic.[6]

According to Freud, man had buried within him certain brutal and sometimes overmastering instincts which caused him to act as he did. Freud said that man's trouble stemmed from these instincts and the effort of man to repress[7] them. I wish you to mark that theory very well. It was given without proof or the phenomena of observation necessary to prove it. It was given as a lucky guess, maybe, but it was given. Freud never

---

3. **Babylon:** the capital of an ancient empire called Babylonia which was located in southwest Asia and flourished from 2100 to 538 B.C.
4. **Chaldea:** province of Babylonia, the ancient empire in what is now southern Iraq.
5. **James Clerk Maxwell:** (1831–1879) Scottish physicist whose research and discoveries advanced the knowledge of electromagnetism, color perception and other areas.
6. **mystic:** a person who practices mysticism, the beliefs or practices of those who claim to have experiences based on intuition, meditation, etc., of a spiritual nature, by which they learn truths not known by ordinary people.
7. **repress:** keep under control, check or suppress (desires, feelings, actions, tears, etc.).

handled or measured one of these instincts. He said they were there. That is all he said. That theory was added to the bulk of data already accumulated about the human mind.

Suppose I were to tell you that the basic savage instincts of man—the instincts which make him kill and murder and engage in war—existed in such a state that they could be handled, measured, experienced, with a clarity and precision never before attained in this field. That would be a good science, wouldn't it?

Techniques of application exist very adequate to handle these basic and savage instincts, because that is what they are.

Living with the beasts of the jungle and caught at every hand[8] by death and terror, early man couldn't do anything else but develop a brutal reaction. Maybe he might have been *good* before he started to hit the physical universe, but by the time he hit that, he hit tooth and claw, and murder and war were commonplace. He had to kill to live, and he kept on killing.

Now he has a civilization all laid out that should run according to plan and everybody ought to be free and happy and we shouldn't have any laws, and the prisons ought to be empty and there shouldn't be any insanity and there ought to be plenty to eat. This would be a real control of the environment and man, and we don't have that.

What is standing in the road? These brutal and

---

8. **at every hand:** on all sides; in every direction.

savage instincts, maybe? Something man picked up when he was swinging from trees or hiding in caves or even earlier. Kill, tooth and claw—these instincts, perhaps, he has carried forward with him into his modern, civilized world, until you can actually get a man to consent to go out and be trained to have a rifle put in his hand and shoot another man in the name of something or other.

Man hasn't been able to escape his heritage. We found that out. He is grasping wildly today for some method of restraining the brutality of his fellows or even himself. He looks toward government—community government, state government, city, national and even an international government—to restrain the brutality of his fellows and maybe even himself.

Perhaps he is motivated in all that brutality by all the crimes which lie back in the yesterdays, which remain, somehow, as built-in instincts.

Freud said brutal instincts exist. He said that man had to fight them down and repress them, that this conflict caused human and social illness. Well, what are the instincts? Where are they? How brutal are they? How does one go about getting rid of them? For, logically, if something exists, one can certainly do something about it.

Further, how would man react if he *did* get rid of these instincts? Would all of his ambitions, his freedom, his forces, his imagination be gone? Or would they be better? Would he have more imagination and more freedom and more power and strength and better health if these instincts were gone? That question has to be answered too.

It is all very well to have a lot of theories. Theories are wonderful things. As long as you don't have phenomena, you can have all the theories you want to. That is a rule in engineering. You get a theory and then you try to apply the thing, and if it doesn't apply to the physical universe you throw it out and get another theory.

Unfortunately, the field of the mind has been able to accumulate a *terrific* number of theories without running into any phenomena to prove or disprove them.

If we have a theory about this brutal instinct, we had certainly better find out if it is a good theory or a bad theory, if it is provable, if the phenomena is there.

Unless you have phenomena to back this up, unless you can weigh and measure these things—and measure them accurately—they still remain in a big state of "up in the air."[9] Who has any authority to say what theory is valid? Nobody has any authority to *say* what theory is valid.

If man were found to be good and free when the instinct was lifted, and if he could reach inside of himself and lift this instinct to kill and to be brutal and savage, *then* you could solve the problem.

I hate such words as *instincts* because they are a big indefiniteness. Can you measure an instinct with

9. up in the air: not settled; not decided.

amperes[10] and watts?[11] Can you feel one and see one? Yes, you can. We can now measure them in amperes and watts, look at them, sort them, tell you how long they are and how wide they are and how thick they are. Can we eradicate them from the mind? Yes, just like you would burn up a piece of cloth.

Is man healthier and better with them gone? Is he then able to cope with the universe better? Is he able to act better? Is he able to handle himself better? Is he more social? Is he happier? Is he freer? Is he more individualistic? Because you would lose if he weren't those things. You don't want prefrontal-lobotomied[12] slaves—not in man. You want man to be as free as you can possibly make him.

Fortunately—no credit to anybody—when you pick up these instincts he becomes free and he becomes social and he is able to cope with his environment, and he no longer wants to go around and steal, murder, burn or engage in war. Fortunately.

Man is basically good, and between him and this goodness lies a savage and twisted past. He inherited it from centuries of being, centuries of savageness, and the instincts he had to wear as a primitive and as a savage. He has still got them, and they are there and they are fully and wholly on record.

---

10. **amperes:** the standard units for measuring the strength of an electric current.
11. **watts:** units of electrical power.
12. **prefrontal-lobotomied:** subjected to a prefrontal lobotomy, a surgical procedure in which the frontal lobes are separated from the rest of the brain by cutting the connecting nerve fibers. Used by psychiatry supposedly for the purpose of relieving symptoms of mental illness.

Oddly enough, his basic instinct is to protect and help his fellows, himself. He is not a single, all-out-for-number-one character. But he gets these instincts, and they get in his road and they make him *act* like he is all out for himself. There isn't a person who hasn't tried very, very hard to help their fellow man—not one. Also, there isn't one who hasn't been cuffed[13] for doing it.

That is a funny thing. Here we have a creature who wants to help, who wants to be unified with his fellows, who wants to be loved, who wants to be secure and at the same time adventurous, who wants to be a unified civilization. We have him all torn apart inside himself and amongst his groups so that all he does about it, really, is nag and rave and commit war.

You take the savage, antisocial impulse of man—any man, woman or child—away and he is freer to act, because now he *can* act. Before, every time he acted he said, "Well—gulp! Maybe this is the time I killed Ug." Here is this impulse that he developed somewhere back on the track:[14] It is some kind of an instinct that he has carried along his protoplasm line[15] or genetic line.[16] You take these instincts up—you can find them—and a man's intelligence sometimes as much as doubles.

He can't even let himself think as clearly as he

---

13. **cuffed:** struck; beat.
14. **track:** *see* **time track** in the glossary.
15. **protoplasm line:** *see* **genetic line** below.
16. **genetic line:** the protoplasm (essential living matter of cells) line. It consists of the total of incidents which have occurred during the evolution of the body itself.

could, because think what he might think about. There is something there that he shouldn't think about and so he limits his own thinking capacity.

We have found the instincts and the lid on the unconscious mind[17]—the subconscious[18] or whatever you want to call it—and the content of that subconscious mind. That is interesting, but it is even more interesting that when one takes away the force and power of a brutal self, the individual's nature is changed so that he is much more successful than he was before. He is the same person he always was, but he is the person who is no longer repressed, held down, unsuccessful, unhappy. He is safe to *trust* something to. You could go out and give such a man an atom bomb and you could say, "Here." He would say, "My golly, somebody is liable to do something with this. I'd better take awful good care that this thing doesn't get loose *anyplace.*"

Perhaps, now, it may be possible in an overwrought[19] world to do something about the criminals, the insane, about war, the antisocial hatred man feels for man. But it is something of a race, too. It is a race with something my classmates invented—a something called an atom bomb.

---

17. **unconscious mind:** a term from psychoanalysis. It is said to be the sum of all thoughts, memories, impulses, desires, feelings, etc., of which the individual is not conscious but which influence his emotions and behavior. In actuality, the "unconscious" is the sum of all a man's bad experiences and nothing more mysterious than that. In Dianetics and Scientology it is called the reactive mind. *See also* **reactive** and **reactive mind** in the glossary.
18. **subconscious:** *see* **unconscious mind** above.
19. **overwrought:** extremely or excessively excited or agitated.

The way to make man reasonable should have preceded atomic fission.[20] It has come up concurrently with it. Thus it is a vital race. One does not know who will win. Can we do something for the savage in civilized garb before he ruins this world and all man? That is a question which the future must answer. I cannot do more than the work I have done and to publish and make available what has been done.

Every facility which we have and all the knowledge which we have gained is at your disposal. It is at your disposal to treat your crippled, your ill, your infirm, to improve you, to make crime a thing of yesterday, to banish war forever. But it is up to you.

*

20. **fission:** the act of cleaving or splitting into parts. *Nuclear fission* is the splitting of the nucleus of an atom into nuclei of lighter atoms, accompanied by the release of energy. The word comes from Latin *fission,* meaning "a splitting, dividing."

23 THE THIRD PARTY LAW

23

THE THIRD
PARTY LAW

I have for a very long time studied the causes of violence and conflict amongst individuals and nations.

If Chaldea could vanish, if Babylon could turn to dust, if Egypt could become a badlands,[1] if Sicily could have 160 prosperous cities and be a looted ruin before the year zero and a near desert ever since—and all this in *spite* of all the work and wisdom and good wishes and intent of human beings—then it must follow as the dark follows sunset that something must be unknown to man concerning all his works and ways. And that this something must be so deadly and so pervasive as to destroy all his ambitions and his chances long before their time.

Such a thing would have to be some natural law unguessed at by himself.

And there *is* such a law, apparently, that answers these conditions of being deadly, unknown and embracing all activities.

The law would seem to be:

> *A third party must be present and unknown in
> every quarrel for a conflict to exist.*

or

---

1. **badlands:** any section of barren land where rapid erosion has cut the loose, dry soil or soft rocks into strange shapes.

> *For a quarrel to occur, an unknown third party must be active in producing it between two potential opponents.*

or

> *While it is commonly believed to take two to make a fight, a third party must exist and must develop it for actual conflict to occur.*

It is very easy to see that two in conflict are fighting. They are very visible. What is harder to see or suspect is that a third party existed and actively promoted the quarrel.

The usually unsuspected and "reasonable" third party, the bystander who denies any part of it, *is* the one that brought the conflict into existence in the first place.

The hidden third party, seeming at times to be a supporter of only one side, is to be found as the instigator.

This is a useful law on many dynamics.

It is the cause of war.

One sees two fellows shouting bad names at each other, sees them come to blows. No one else is around. So *they*, of course, "caused the fight." But there *was* a third party.

Tracing these down, one comes upon incredible data. That is the trouble. The incredible is too easily rejected. One way to hide things is to make them incredible.

Clerk A and Messenger B have been arguing. They blaze into direct conflict. Each blames the other. *Neither one is correct and so the quarrel does not resolve since its true cause is not established.*

One looks into such a case *thoroughly*. He finds the incredible. The wife of Clerk A has been sleeping with Messenger B and complaining alike to both about the other.

Farmer J and Rancher K have been tearing each other to pieces for years in continual conflict. There are obvious, logical reasons for the fight. Yet it continues and does not resolve. A close search finds Banker L who, due to their losses in the fighting, is able to loan each side money while keeping the quarrel going, and who will get their lands completely if both lose.

It goes larger. The revolutionary forces and the Russian government were in conflict in 1917. The reasons are so many the attention easily sticks on them. But only when Germany's official state papers were captured in World War II was it revealed that Germany had promoted the revolt and financed *Lenin*[2] to spark it off, even sending him into Russia in a blacked-out train!

One looks over "personal" quarrels, group conflicts, national battles and one finds, if he searches, the third party, unsuspected by both combatants or, if suspected at all, brushed off as "fantastic." Yet careful documentation finally affirms it.

This datum is fabulously useful.

---

2. **Lenin:** Vladimir I. Lenin (1870–1924), Russian communist leader. He was an agitator for socialism. During World War I he urged socialists in all countries to rise against their own governments, and he assumed leadership of the Russian Revolution in 1917.

In marital quarrels the *correct* approach of anyone counseling is to get both parties to carefully search out the *third* party. They may come to many *reasons* at first. These reasons are not beings. One is looking for a third *party,* an actual *being.* When both find the third party and establish proof, that will be the end of the quarrel.

Sometimes two parties, quarreling, suddenly decide to elect a being to blame. This stops the quarrel. Sometimes it is not the right being and more quarrels thereafter occur.

Two nations at each other's throats should each seek conference with the other to sift out and locate the actual third party. They will always find one if they look, and they *can* find the right one. As it will be found to exist in fact.

There are probably many technical approaches one could develop and outline in this matter.

There are many odd phenomena connected with it. An accurately spotted third party is usually not fought at all by either party but only shunned.

Marital conflicts are common. Marriages can be saved by both parties really sorting out *who* caused the conflicts. There may have been, in the whole history of the marriage, several, but only one at a time.

Quarrels between an individual and an organization are nearly always caused by an individual third party or a third group. The organization and the individual should get together and isolate the third party by displaying to each other all the data they each have been fed.

Rioters and governments alike could be brought back to agreement could one get representatives of both to give each other what they have been told by *whom*.

Such conferences have tended to deal only in recrimina-tions[3] or conditions or abuses. They must deal in beings only in order to succeed.

This theory might be thought to assert also that there are no bad conditions that cause conflict. There are. But these are usually *remedial by conference unless a third party is promoting conflict.*

In history we have a very foul opinion of the past because it is related by recriminations of two opponents and has not spotted the third party.

"Underlying causes" of war should read "hidden promoters."

There are no conflicts which cannot be resolved unless the true promoters of them remain hidden.

This is the natural law the ancients and moderns alike did not know.

And not knowing it, being led off into "reasons," whole civilizations have died.

It is worth knowing.

It is worth working with in any situation where one is trying to bring peace.

<hr>

3. recriminations: counteraccusations; accusations brought in turn by the accused against the accuser.

24 JUSTICE

24

JUSTICE

What *is* justice?

"The quality of mercy is not strained[1]—it droppeth as the gentle rain from heaven . . ." may be poetic, but it is not definitive. It does, however, demonstrate that even in Shakespeare's time men were adrift on the subject of justice, injustice, severity and mercy.

People speak of an action as unjust or an action as just. What do they mean? Yet, unless we can understand exactly what is meant by these terms, we certainly cannot undertake to evaluate the actions of individuals, communities and nations. For the lack of an ability to so evaluate, misunderstandings come about which have, in the past, led to combative personal relationships and, on the international scene, to war. An individual or a nation fails or refuses to understand the measures taken by another or fails to fall within the agreement of the pattern to which others are accustomed and chaos results.

In Scientology the following definitions now exist:

Justice—the impartial administration of the laws of the land in accordance with the extant level of the severity–mercy ratio of the people.

---

1. **"The quality of mercy is not strained . . .":** the beginning line of a passage from act four, scene one of Shakespeare's play *The Merchant of Venice* (1596–1597). *See also* **Shakespeare** in the glossary.

Laws—the codified agreements of the people crystallizing their customs and representing their believed-in necessities of conduct.

Mercy—a lessening away from the public's acceptance of discipline necessary to guarantee their mutual security.

Severity—an increase in that discipline believed necessary by the people to guarantee their security.

Injustice—failure to administer existing law.

Equity—any civil procedure holding citizens responsible to citizens which delivers decision to persons in accordance with the general expectancy in such cases.

Rights—the franchises[2] of citizenship according to existing codes.

When laws are not derived from custom or when a new law contravenes[3] an uncancelled old law, exact law becomes confused and injustice is then inevitable.

Basic justice can occur only when codified law or a majority-held custom exists.

Observing these definitions, jurisprudence only then becomes possible. Law courts, legislatures[4] and legislation[5] become confused, as nothing is possible in the absence of an understanding of such principles.

---

2. **franchises:** the privileges or rights granted by a government.
3. **contravenes:** goes against; opposes; conflicts with; violates.
4. **legislatures:** bodies of persons given the responsibility and power to make laws for countries or states.
5. **legislation:** law or laws made by legislatures for countries or states.

Laws which do not derive from agreement amongst the society, which we call custom, are unenforceable unless there is then a widespread agreement that this is customary in the society. No matter how many police are hired, no matter the purity of prose with which the legislation is written, no matter the signatures occurring on the enforcing document, the public will not obey that law. Similarly, when a government acts to ignore certain basic customs amongst the people and refuses to enforce them, that government then finds itself in a state of civil turmoil with its people on that subject. We can look at any public–government battle and discover that it stems exactly from a violation of these principles.

An understanding on the part of a nation of the difficulties of another is necessary to a continued peace. When one nation begins to misunderstand the motives and justices conceived necessary by another nation, stress sets up which eventually leads to war, all too often.

Whenever there is an excessive commotion amongst a people against its government, the government is then invited to act as an opponent to the people. If a government is acting toward its people as though it were an opponent of the people and not a member of the team, it becomes obvious that many of these points must exist in the law codes of the country which violate the customs of the people. Wherever such a point exists, turbulence results.

And that is justice.

✾

25 WHAT IS KNOWLEDGE?

25

WHAT IS
KNOWLEDGE?

Knowledge itself is certainty; knowledge is *not* data. Knowingness itself is certainty. Sanity is certainty, providing only that that certainty does not fall beyond the conviction of another when he views it.

To obtain a certainty one must be able to observe. But what is the level of certainty required? And what is the level of observation required for a certainty or a knowledge to exist?

If a man can stand before a tree and by sight, touch or other perception know that he is confronting a tree and be able to perceive its form and be quite sure he is confronting a tree, we have the level of certainty required. If the man will not look at the tree or, although it is observably a tree to others, if he discovers it to be a blade of grass or a sun, then he is below the level of certainty required. Some other person, helpfully inclined, would have to direct his perception to the tree until the man perceived without duress that it was indeed a tree he confronted. That is the only level of certainty required in order to qualify knowledge. For knowledge is observation and is given to those who would look.

In order to obtain knowledge and certainty, it is necessary to be able to observe, in fact, three universes in which there could be trees. The first of these is one's own universe; one should be able to create for his own observation, in its total form for total perception, a tree. The second universe would be the material universe, which is the universe of matter, energy, space and time, which is the common meeting ground of all of us. The third universe is actually a class of universes, which could be called "the other fellow's universe," for he and all the class of "other fellows" have universes of their own.

A doctor, for instance, may seem entirely certain of the cause of some disease, yet it depends upon the doctor's certainty for the layman to accept that cause of the disease. That penicillin cures certain things is a certainty to the doctor even when penicillin suddenly and inexplicably fails to cure something. Any inexplicable failure introduces an uncertainty, which thereafter removes the subject from the realm of an easily obtained certainty.

We have here, then, a parallel between certainty and sanity.

The less certain the individual on any subject, the less sane he could be said to be upon that subject; the less certain he is of what he views in the material universe, what he views in his own or the other fellow's universe, the less sane he could be said to be.

The road to sanity is demonstrably the road to increasing certainty. Starting at any level, it is only necessary to obtain a fair degree of certainty on the material universe to improve considerably one's beingness.

Above that, one obtains some certainty of his own universe and some certainty of the other fellow's universe.

Certainty, then, is clarity of observation. Of course, above this, vitally so, is certainty in creation. Here is the artist, here is the master, here is the very great spirit.

As one advances he discovers that what he first perceived as a certainty can be considerably improved. Thus we have certainty as a gradient scale.[1] It is not an absolute, but it is defined as the certainty that one perceives or the certainty that one creates what one perceives or the certainty that there is perception. Sanity and perception, certainty and perception, knowledge and observation are, then, all of a kind, and amongst them we have sanity.

The road into uncertainty is the road toward psychosomatic[2] illness, doubts, anxieties, fears, worries and vanishing awareness. As awareness is decreased, so does certainty decrease.

It is very puzzling to people at higher levels of awareness why people behave toward them as they do; such higher-level people have not realized that they are not seen, much less understood. People at low levels of awareness do not observe, but substitute for observation

---

1. **gradient scale:** a scale of condition graduated from zero to infinity. On a scale of certainty, everything above zero or center would be more and more certain, approaching an infinite certainty, and everything below zero or center would be more and more uncertain, approaching an infinite uncertainty. Absolutes are considered to be unobtainable.

2. **psychosomatic:** *psycho* refers to mind and *somatic* refers to body; the term *psychosomatic* means the mind making the body ill or illnesses which have been created physically within the body by derangement of the mind.

preconceptions, evaluation and suppositions, and even physical pain by which to attain their certainties.

The mistaken use of shock by the ancient Greek upon the insane, the use of whips in old Bedlam,[3] all sought to deliver sufficient certainty to the insane to cause them to be less insane.

Certainty delivered by blow and punishment is a nonself-determined certainty. It is productive of stimulus-response[4] behavior. At a given stimulus, a dog who has been beaten, for instance, will react invariably, providing he has been sufficiently beaten; but if he has been beaten too much, the stimulus will result only in confused bewilderment. Thus certainty delivered by blows, by applied force, eventually brings about a certainty as absolute as one could desire—total unawareness. Unconsciousness itself is a certainty which is sought by many individuals who have failed repeatedly to reach any high level of awareness certainty. These people, then, desire an unawareness certainty. So it seems that the thirst for certainty can lead one into oblivion if one seeks it as an effect.

An uncertainty is the product of two certainties. One of these is a conviction, whether arrived at by observation (causative) or by a blow (effected). The other is a negative certainty. One can be sure that something is and one can be sure that something is not. He can be sure that there is something, no matter what it is, present,

---

3. **Bedlam:** an old insane asylum (in full, St. Mary of Bethlehem) in London, infamous for the brutal ill-treatment inflicted upon the insane.
4. **stimulus-response:** of or having to do with a certain stimulus automatically giving a certain response.

and that there is nothing present. These two certainties commingling, create a condition of uncertainty known as "maybe." A "maybe" continues to be held in suspense in an individual's mind simply because he cannot decide whether it is nothing or something. He grasps and holds the certainties each time he has been given evidence or has made the decision that it is a somethingness and each time he has come to suppose that it is a nothingness. Where these two certainties of something and nothing are concerned with, and can vitally influence, one's continuance in a state of beingness, or where one merely supposes they can influence such a state of beingness, a condition of anxiety arises. Thus anxiety, indecision, uncertainty, a state of "maybe" can exist only in the presence of poor observation or the inability to observe.

※

26 MAN FROM MUD

26

MAN
FROM MUD

Lt is often amusing to catch
"science" out[1] in its pompous parade of authority and
gadgetry, and often amazing that some fields are not
arrested for "false pretenses."

Amongst those present in this parade is the modern
"biologist" with his modern "Man from Mud" theory.

According to the professors in this "field," man
is an animal who arose as a result of a spontaneous
accident from a "sea of ammonia" and by the stages of
development called "evolution," arrived at the proud
estate[2] of a two-legged wog.[3] This is the theory taught as
the theory in most universities today.

So to those who resent people calling Scientology
theory to account[4] as "wild," look at that "Man from
Mud" theory, a backbone of biology, psychology and
psychiatry to name a few. It is excruciatingly funny.

The idea of an "accidental" "combination of chemicals" coming alive, in all places, in a "sea of ammonia"

---

1. **catch (someone or something) out:** catch or discover (someone or something) in deceit or in error.
2. **estate:** social status or rank.
3. **wog:** *(Scientology slang)* a common, ordinary, run-of-the-mill, garden-variety humanoid, by which we mean an individual that considers that he is a body and does not know that he is there as a spirit at all.
4. **calling to account:** blaming; reprimanding.

and then evolving into a thinking being of the complexity of man is more ridiculous than a Joe Miller joke book.[5]

Yet the bearded ones will viciously flunk a student who dares to disagree.

Biology means "life science" and is nothing of the sort by its own practice. It is at best "cytology," a science dealing with body and vegetable cells as it is a subject entirely devoted to *cells*, not to life as everyone else thinks of it. So even its name is false.

And on the subject of false names, modern "psychology," using "biology" as its excuse for fixation on brains, dares preempt[6] the word *psychology*. This means "soul, study of" (psyche = soul). But in their classrooms all they study is *brains*. They think that as man arose in a sea of ammonia by spontaneous combustion,[7] they therefore have to concentrate on *brain cells*, feed them chemicals or cut them up to get at *life*. They are not psyche-ologists at all but at best "brainologists." If you ask one to define *psychology* as a word he says (and so do his texts) that he doesn't know what his *science title* means.

This stops him right there. So he is a fake. That's

---

5. **Joe Miller joke book:** a book of old or worn-out jokes, erroneously attributed to Joe Miller (1684–1738), an English actor and comedian. The book was actually published a year after his death and went through many printings. Timeworn jests are sometimes called "a Joe Miller."

6. **preempt:** take over.

7. **spontaneous combustion:** the process of catching fire as a result of heat generated by internal chemical action. Used satirically in this book to describe *spontaneous generation*, the theory, now discredited, that living organisms can originate in nonliving matter independently of other living matter.

why he loves to call everyone else a "fake." He knows *he* is one. He didn't even know IQ[8] could change until we came along. "Man's IQ never changes," says his pre-Scientology texts. After she read Scientology materials, a psychologist in the late 1950s got a national prize for saying IQ changed. She couldn't change it but she said it changed. Afterwards universities got even with us by saying IQ didn't exist. As this was about all a psychologist did—measure IQ (and study rats)—they wiped themselves out as a profession.

Psychiatry has to get at brains with shock, knives, ice picks because as man came from mud as a cell, the think-cell must be what makes him go mad, so if one cuts or damages the "cells that think" then man will become sane. Doing these inhuman crimes, their statistic of insanity has risen like a rocket. Yet they never question for a moment the basic theory on which they "operate" despite no gains in their "profession"—and do a great deal of harm. So that's where the "Man from Mud" theory took them.

In Scientology we raise IQ easily and do all sorts of things that used to be called miracles solely because we know man is a spiritual being inhabiting a flesh body. We don't worry about the cells because man isn't one. So we get results. Because we operate on truth and don't indulge in popular theories just because Priest Scientist says some lie in a loud university chant, slavishly quoted by the newspapers!

---

8. IQ: *Intelligence Quotient:* a number intended to indicate a person's level of intelligence. Intelligence quotient (IQ) ratings are a measure of an individual's capacity for learning something new; they are a scale based upon how old in years a person has become compared to how "old" he is mentally.

We are not popular with the old witch doctors—the biologists, psychologists and psychiatrists—because as we go on we show them up as frauds.

Our truths speak far louder than their curses. And our *results* prove our truths.

If we succeed fully they will be looked on by one and all as humbugs.[9] And to their already colorful crimes they have added the crime of seeking by libel and slander to suppress truth. Such people seldom prosper.

But about this "Man from Mud" theory, where did it come from? What great Einstein of biology burped it up?

Why, no great Einstein of biology or psychology or psychiatry ever had any part in the origin of the "Man from Mud" theory.

Far from having come from "science," the "Man from Mud" theory was taken by these scientists from a body of religious demonology[10] and foisted off on man as "modern thought." What you'd expect from fakes.

What religious demonology? Why, the Egyptian, of course. In the *Larousse Encyclopaedia of Mythology*, the standard work, we find in column 1, page 11, under "Divinities attached to the Ennead of Heliopolis[11] and the Family of Osiris[12]" the following paragraph:

---

9. **humbugs:** persons who are not what they claim to be; impostors.
10. **demonology:** the study of demons or of beliefs about them.
11. **Ennead of Heliopolis:** the group of nine gods (*Ennead*) of ancient Egyptian religion originating from the city of Heliopolis, one of the principal religious centers of the period.
12. **Osiris:** one of the chief gods of ancient Egypt, ruler of the lower world and judge of the dead. He represented good and productivity and is identified with the Nile.

Nun (or Nu) is chaos, the primordial[13] ocean in which before the creation lay the germs of all things and all beings.

These "scientific" pots[14] who are calling everyone fakes might have done a bit better than to try to foist off on the world mere religious superstition as the scientific basis on which all their whole "science" is laid.

Man from mud?

The only mud connected with man is the mud slung by pompous fakes trying to defend the hopeless cause of keeping man in ignorance of the truth.

These are the fellows who call Scientology theory "wild" and "science fiction." At least we're more modern than the earliest religious demonology of Egypt!

How can one take such people seriously?

※

---

13. **primordial:** pertaining to or existing at or from the very beginning.
14. **pots:** *(British slang)* persons of importance.

27 THE PSYCHIATRIST AT WORK

27

THE PSYCHIATRIST AT WORK

Scientologists are often fought by psychiatry. They are often called upon to handle psychiatric abuses. Scientologists should know some facts about psychiatry.

PAIN ASSOCIATION

As a technical action, it is of interest to anyone to know that pain and ideas is a basic "therapy" used down the years by psychiatrists and such lot.

The practice is very general and very old.

The person is made to associate his "wrong ideas" with pain so that he "will not have these ideas," or will be "prevented from doing those things."

A crude current example is to electric shock a person every time he smokes a cigarette. After several "treatments," he is supposed to associate the pain with the idea and so "give up smoking."

Homosexual tendencies are also so "treated."

In earlier times alcoholism was "cured" by putting poison in drinks so drinking would make the person violently ill so he would "stop it."

Examples of this are all over the time track.[1]

The mechanism is "If you get this idea, you will feel this pain," ZAP!

Basically, this is the action of an implanter.[2]

Current use of it will be encountered where psychiatry has been busy implanting.

This is a pinnacle, an all, of psychiatric "treatment."

Another version of it is drugs. Make the person too torpid (sluggish) to have *any* ideas. The motto of this is "too dead to act." Institutions are emptied by hooking psychotics and "community psychiatry" exists "to make them take their pills," in short, to keep them hooked. This started the current drug craze that spread into "illegal" drugs.

Scientologists will encounter this with growing frequency as the business of it is so big that one group spends 12 billion in advertising alone per year! This is the Rockefeller[3] drug cartel.[4] They also spend vast sums in lobbying[5] parliaments.[6]

---

1. **time track:** the consecutive record of mental image pictures which accumulate through a person's life or lives. It is very exactly dated. The time track is the entire sequence of "now" incidents, complete with all sense messages, picked up by a person during his whole existence.
2. **implanter:** one who administers an *implant*, an enforced command or series of commands installed in the reactive mind below the awareness level of the individual to cause him to react or behave in a prearranged way without his "knowing it."
3. **Rockefeller:** of or having to do with the Rockefeller family or its international financial interests. Originally founded in the oil business by John D. Rockefeller (1839–1937), his heirs have continued to expand its influence in many areas internationally.
4. **cartel:** a large group of business firms that agree to operate as a monopoly, especially to regulate prices and production.
5. **lobbying:** influencing lawmakers in voting for or against certain laws, in order to benefit a special group.
6. **parliaments:** highest lawmaking bodies in some countries.

OBSESSION

Most "got to's," or obsessions, come from pain association or drug association.

People in pain or drugged can become obsessed with *doing* the idea.

What the psychiatrist does not care to publicize is that his "cures" are implantings with compulsive ideas.

The smoker so treated now *must* smoke but *can't* smoke. These two things are opposed. That is known as frustration—a form of insanity.

Must reach–can't reach, must withdraw–can't withdraw is total basic insanity.

Thus, psychiatry is *making* insane people.

This is why the insanity statistic is soaring and why the crime statistic is on a wild climb.

The psychiatrist, if he handled his field well and did really effective work, would have a *declining* insanity and crime statistic.

That the psychiatrist and his "technology" has been in charge during the whole period of these alarming statistics is ignored by governments.

The psychiatrist argues that he needs more money and more practitioners. But he gets money by the billion. The state has to totally support them because the public will have nothing to do with them.

Psychoanalysis costs 9,000 pounds[7] for a full and ineffective course, takes five years, 30 percent suicide in the first three months.

Psychiatric treatment runs five times the total cost of every course, grade[8] and action available in Scientology organizations.

SKILL LEVEL

Any beginning Scientologist knows more and can do more about the mind than any psychiatrist.

There is no real level of comparison since psychiatry as used is a destructive technology.

Under a "drug treatment" engram[9] you often find savage electric shocks of execution strength buried.

It is doubtful if one could watch an electric shock "treatment" without vomiting.

In "neurosurgery"[10] the ice pick is used to rip and tear up people's brains.

Holes are drilled in skulls and the brain sliced up.

No evidence exists that this ever helped anyone, but it makes incurable invalids.

---

7. **pounds:** the basic unit of money in the United Kingdom; also called *pounds sterling.*
8. **grade:** a series of processes which are run on a person with the purpose of bringing him to a particular state of release (what occurs when a person separates from his reactive mind or some part of it).
9. **engram:** a mental image picture which is a recording of a time of physical pain and unconsciousness. It must by definition have impact or injury as part of its contents.
10. **neurosurgery:** surgery of the brain or other nerve tissue.

Illegal seizure of anyone and his torture is legal in most "civilized countries."

MASTERS

The psychiatrist has masters. His principal organization, World Federation of Mental Health, and its members, the National Associations of Mental Health, the "American" Psychiatric Association and the "American" Psychological Association, are directly connected to Russia.

Even the British broadcasting company[11] has stated that psychiatry and the KGB (Russian secret police) operate in direct collusion.[12]

A member of the WFMH sits on every major "Advisory Council" of the US government, to name one government.

Ministers of health or health authorities are members of the National Association or the WFMH.

The psychiatrist has masters.

DOCUMENTATION

All these statements are the subject of total documentation in the hands of Scientology.

---

11. **British broadcasting company:** reference to the *British Broadcasting Corporation,* the government-sponsored radio and television company of the United Kingdom. Often abbreviated as *BBC.*
12. **collusion:** secret agreement for fraudulent or illegal purposes; conspiracy.

SUMMARY

The Scientology auditor in auditing uncovers considerable data in former psychiatric cases.

Further, an auditor can put to rights[13] a case so abused unless a fatal injury has been done.

As psychiatry circulates rumors about Scientologists and attempts to discourage the use of Scientology, it is only fair for Scientologists to know exactly the status of psychiatry and psychology as used today.

It goes without saying that the savagery and fraud of psychiatry must cease and that Scientologists must encourage in state and public and through all their connections displacing psychiatric abuses with sane auditing.

※

---

13. **put to rights:** put into good or proper condition or order.

Nothing in THIS WORLD lasts FOREVER

So maybe it's time to go for something out of THIS WORLD...

Now that you have read this book, you have a new way of viewing life.

Knowing what life is and why you are here makes problems easier to solve. That's why learning SCIENTOLOGY® is such a stellar idea.

SCIENTOLOGY takes raw human ability and brings out the brilliance that was there all along. Hundreds of thousands of individuals tested show increased IQ scores resulting in bettered aptitude and decision-making abilities. Contrary to what you have been told, IQ can be increased, we have the graphs to prove it.

To find out more about SCIENTOLOGY fill out this card. Mail it in. We'll send you more information about SCIENTOLOGY and a free personality test.

SCIENTOLOGY results in TOTAL FREEDOM. That's freedom that lasts forever.

It'll help you reach the star you are looking for – no matter what galaxy it's in...

☐ YES! I want more information about SCIENTOLOGY and a FREE personality test.

Name

Address

City

State

Zip

Phone

SEND THIS CARD TODAY!
or for more information, call toll free 1-800-334-5433

© 1997 BPI. All Rights Reserved. SCIENTOLOGY is a trademark and service mark owned by Religious Technology Center and is used with its approval. SCIENTOLOGY applied religious philosophy. Item #3866

28 HONEST PEOPLE HAVE RIGHTS, TOO

28

HONEST PEOPLE HAVE RIGHTS, TOO

After you have achieved a high level of ability, you will be the first to insist upon your rights to live with honest people.

When you know the technology of the mind, you know that it is a mistake to use "individual rights" and "freedom" as arguments to protect those who would only destroy.

Individual rights were not originated to protect criminals but to bring freedom to honest men. Into this area of protection then dived those who needed "freedom" and "individual liberty" to cover their own questionable activities.

Freedom is for honest people. No man who is not himself honest can be free—he is his own trap. When his own deeds cannot be disclosed, then he is a prisoner; he must withhold himself from his fellows and he is a slave to his own conscience. Freedom must be deserved before any freedom is possible.

To protect dishonest people is to condemn them to their own hells. By making "individual rights" a synonym for "protect the criminal" one helps bring about a slave state for all; for where "individual liberty" is abused, an impatience with it arises which at length sweeps us all away. The targets of all disciplinary laws are the few who err. Such laws, unfortunately, also injure and restrict those who do not err. If all were honest, there would be no disciplinary threats.

There is only one way out for a dishonest person—facing up to his own responsibilities in the society and putting himself back into communication with his fellow man, his family, the world at large. By seeking to invoke his "individual rights" to protect himself from an examination of his deeds, he reduces, just that much, the future of individual liberty—for he himself is not free. Yet he infects others who are honest by using *their* right to freedom to protect himself.

Uneasy lies the head that wears a guilty conscience.

And it will lie no more easily by seeking to protect misdeeds by pleas of "freedom means that you must never look at me." The right of a person to survive is directly related to his honesty.

Freedom for man does not mean freedom to injure man. Freedom of speech does not mean freedom to harm by lies.

Man cannot be free while there are those amongst him who are slaves to their own terrors.

The mission of a techno-space society[1] is to subordinate[2] the individual and control him by economic and political duress. The only casualty in a machine age is the individual and his freedom.

To preserve that freedom one must not permit men to hide their evil intentions under the protection of that freedom. To be free, a man must be honest with himself and with his fellows.

---

1. **techno-space society:** a society with technology advanced to the level of being capable of space travel.
2. **subordinate:** make obedient or submissive (to); control; subdue.

If a man uses his own honesty to protest the unmasking of dishonesty, then that man is an enemy of his own freedom.

We can stand in the sun only so long as we do not let the deeds of others bring the darkness.

Freedom is for honest men. Individual liberty exists only for those who have the ability to be free.

Who would punish when he could salvage?

Only a madman would break a wanted object he could repair.

The individual must not die in this machine age— rights or no rights. The criminal and madman must not triumph with their new-found tools of destruction.

The least-free person is the person who cannot reveal his own acts and who protests the revelation of the improper acts of others. On such people will be built a future political slavery where we all have numbers—and our guilt—unless we act.

It is fascinating that blackmail and punishment are the keynotes of all dark operations.[3] What would happen if these two commodities no longer existed? What would happen if all men were free enough to speak? Then, and only then, would you have freedom.

On the day when we can fully trust each other, there will be peace on Earth.

※

---

3. **dark operations**: evil, wicked or harmful activities. Also known as *black operations*.

29 YOU CAN BE RIGHT

29

YOU CAN
BE RIGHT

Rightness and wrongness form a common source of argument and struggle.

The concept of rightness reaches very high and very low on the Tone Scale.

And the effort to be right is the last conscious striving of an individual on the way out. I-am-right-and-they-are-wrong is the lowest concept that can be formulated by an unaware case.

What *is* right and what *is* wrong are not necessarily definable for everyone. These vary according to existing moral codes and disciplines and, before Scientology, despite their use in law as a test of "sanity," had no basis in fact but only in opinion.

In Scientology a more precise definition arose. And the definition became as well the true definition of an overt act. An overt act is not just injuring someone or something: An overt act is an act of omission or commission which does the least good for the least number of dynamics or the most harm to the greatest number of dynamics.

Thus, a wrong action is wrong to the degree that it harms the greatest number of dynamics. And a right action is right to the degree that it benefits the greatest number of dynamics.

Many people think that an action is an overt simply because it is destructive. To them all destructive actions or omissions are overt acts. This is not true. For an act of commission or omission to be an overt act it must harm the greater number of dynamics. A failure to destroy can be, therefore, an overt act. Assistance to something that would harm a greater number of dynamics can also be an overt act.

An overt act is something that harms broadly. A beneficial act is something that helps broadly. It can be a beneficial act to harm something that would be harmful to the greater number of dynamics.

Harming everything and helping everything alike can be overt acts. Helping certain things and harming certain things alike can be beneficial acts.

The idea of not harming anything and helping everything are alike rather mad. It is doubtful if you would think helping enslavers was a beneficial action and equally doubtful if you would consider the destruction of a disease an overt act.

In the matter of being right or being wrong, a lot of muddy thinking can develop. There are no absolute rights or absolute wrongs. And being right does not consist of being unwilling to harm, and being wrong does not consist only of not harming.

There is an irrationality about "being right"

which not only throws out the validity of the legal test of sanity but also explains why some people do very wrong things and insist they are doing right.

The answer lies in an impulse, inborn in everyone, to *try to be right*. This is an insistence which rapidly becomes divorced from right action. And it is accompanied by an effort to make others wrong, as we see in hypercritical cases. A being who is apparently unconscious is *still* being right and making others wrong. It is the last criticism.

We have seen a "defensive person" explaining away the most flagrant wrongnesses. This is "justification" as well. Most explanations of conduct, no matter how far-fetched, seem perfectly right to the person making them since he or she is only asserting self-rightness and other-wrongness.

We have long said that that which is not admired tends to persist. If no one admires a person for being right, then that person's "brand of being right" will persist, no matter how mad it sounds. Scientists who are aberrated cannot seem to get many theories. They do not because they are more interested in insisting on their own odd rightnesses than they are in finding truth. Thus, we get strange "scientific truths" from men who should know better, including the late Einstein. Truth is built by those who have the breadth and balance to see also where they're wrong.

You have heard some very absurd arguments out among the crowd. Realize that the speaker was more interested in *asserting* his or her own rightness than in *being right.*

A thetan[1] *tries* to be right and *fights* being wrong. This is without regard to being right *about* something or to do actual right. It is an *insistence* which has no concern with a rightness of conduct.

One tries to be right *always,* right down to the last spark.

How, then, is one ever wrong?

It is this way:

One does a wrong action, accidentally or through oversight. The wrongness of the action or inaction is then in conflict with one's necessity to be right. So one then may continue and repeat the wrong action to prove it is right.

This is a fundamental of aberration. All wrong actions are the result of an error followed by an insistence on having been right. Instead of righting the error (which would involve being wrong) one insists the error was a right action and so repeats it.

As a being goes down scale, it is harder and harder to admit having been wrong. Nay,[2] such an admission

---

1. **thetan:** the person himself—not his body or his name, the physical universe, his mind or anything else; that which is aware of being aware; the identity which is the individual. The term was coined to eliminate any possible confusion with older, invalid concepts. It comes from the Greek letter theta (θ), which the Greeks used to represent *thought* or perhaps *spirit,* to which an *n* is added to make a noun in the modern style used to create words in engineering. It is also θ^n, or "theta to the nth degree," meaning unlimited or vast.

2. **nay:** not only that, but also.

could well be disastrous to any remaining ability or sanity.

For rightness is the stuff of which survival is made. And as one approaches the last ebb[3] of survival, one can only insist on having been right, for to believe for a moment one has been wrong is to court oblivion.

The last defense of any being is "I was right." That applies to anyone. When that defense crumbles, the lights go out.

So we are faced with the unlovely picture of asserted rightness in the face of flagrant wrongness. And any success in making the being realize their wrongness results in an immediate degradation, unconsciousness or, at best, a loss of personality. Pavlov,[4] Freud, psychiatry alike never grasped the delicacy of these facts and so evaluated and punished the criminal and insane into further criminality and insanity.

All justice today contains in it this hidden error—that the last defense is a belief in personal rightness regardless of charges and evidence alike, and that the effort to make another wrong results only in degradation.

But all this would be a hopeless impasse leading

---

3. **ebb:** decline or decay.
4. **Pavlov:** Ivan Petrovich Pavlov (1849–1936), Russian physiologist; noted for behavioral experiments on dogs.

to highly chaotic social conditions were it not for one saving fact:

All repeated and "incurable" wrongnesses stem from the exercise of a last defense: "trying to be right." Therefore, the compulsive wrongness can be cured no matter how mad it may seem or how thoroughly its rightness is insisted upon.

Getting the offender to admit his or her wrongness is to court further degradation and even unconsciousness or the destruction of a being. Therefore, the purpose of punishment is defeated and punishment has minimal workability.

But by getting the offender off the compulsive repetition of the wrongness, one then cures it.

But how?

By rehabilitating the ability to be right!

This has limitless application—in training, in social skills, in marriage, in law, in life.

Example: A wife is always burning dinner. Despite scolding, threats of divorce, anything, the compulsion continues. One can wipe this wrongness out by getting her to explain what is *right* about her cooking. This may well evoke a raging tirade[5] in some extreme cases, but if one flattens[6] the question, that

---

5. **tirade:** a long, vehement speech.
6. **flattens:** carries on with (a process or question) until the question no longer produces a reaction.

all dies away and she happily ceases to burn dinners. Carried to classic[7] proportions, but not entirely necessary to end the compulsion, a moment in the past will be recovered when she accidentally burned a dinner and could not face up to having done a wrong action. To be right she thereafter had to burn dinners.

Go into a prison and find one sane prisoner who says he did wrong. You won't find one. Only the broken wrecks will say so out of terror of being hurt. But even they don't believe they did wrong.

A judge on a bench,[8] sentencing criminals, would be given pause[9] to realize that not one malefactor[10] sentenced really thought he had done wrong and will never believe it in fact, though he may seek to avert wrath by saying so.

The do-gooder crashes into this continually and is given his losses by it.

But marriage, law and crime do not constitute all the spheres of living where this applies. These facts embrace all of life.

The student who can't learn, the worker who can't work, the boss who can't boss are all caught on one side of the right–wrong question. They are being completely one-sided. They are being "last-ditch right." And opposing them, those who would teach

---

7. **classic:** serving as a standard, model or guide.
8. **on a bench:** presiding in a law court; serving as a judge.
9. **be given pause:** be made hesitant or unsure, as from surprise or doubt.
10. **malefactor:** an evildoer or criminal.

them are fixed on the other side, "admit you are wrong." And out of this we get not only no-change but actual degradation where it "wins." But there are no wins in this imbalance, only losses for both.

Beings on the way down don't believe they are wrong because they don't dare believe it. And so they do not change.

You can be right. How? By getting another to explain how he or she is right—until he or she, being less defensive now, can take a less compulsive point of view. You don't have to agree with what they think. You only have to acknowledge what they say. And suddenly they *can* be right.

A lot of things can be done by understanding and using this mechanism. It will take, however, some study of this article before it can be gracefully applied—for all of us are reactive[11] to some degree on this subject.

As Scientologists, we are faced by a frightened society who think they would be wrong if we were found to be right. We need a weapon to correct this. We have one here.

And you can be right, you know. I was probably the first to believe you were, mechanism or no mechanism. The road to rightness is the road to survival. And every person is somewhere on that scale.

---

11. **reactive:** irrational, reacting instead of acting; thinkingness or behavior dictated by the reactive mind rather than the individual's own present time determinism. *See also* **reactive mind** in the glossary.

You can make yourself right, amongst other ways, by making others right enough to afford to change their minds. Then a lot more of us will arrive.

30 WHAT IS GREATNESS?

30

WHAT IS GREATNESS?

The hardest task one can have is to continue to love his fellows despite all reasons he should not.

And the true sign of sanity and greatness is to so continue.

For the one who can achieve this, there is abundant hope.

For those who cannot, there is only sorrow, hatred and despair. And these are not the things of which greatness or sanity or happiness are made.

A primary trap is to succumb to invitations to hate.

There are those who appoint one their executioners. Sometimes for the sake of safety of others it is necessary to act. But it is not necessary also to hate them.

To do one's task without becoming furious at others who seek to prevent one is a mark of greatness—and sanity. And only then can one be happy.

Seeking to achieve any single desirable quality in life is a noble thing. The one most difficult—and most necessary to achieve—is to love one's fellows despite all invitations to do otherwise.

If there is any saintly quality, it is not to forgive. "Forgiveness" accepts the badness of the act. There is no reason to accept it. Further, one has to label the act as bad to forgive it. "Forgiveness" is a much lower-level action and is rather censorious.[1]

True greatness merely refuses to change in the face of bad actions against one—and a truly great person loves his fellows because he understands them.

After all, they are all in the same trap. Some are oblivious of it, some have gone mad because of it, some act like those who betrayed them. But all, all are in the same trap—the generals, the street sweepers, the presidents, the insane. They act the way they do because they are all subject to the same cruel pressures of this universe.

Some of us are subject to those pressures and still go on doing our jobs. Others have long since succumbed and rave and torture and strut like the demented[2] souls they are.

To resave some of them is a dangerous undertaking. Were you to approach many ruling heads in the world and offer to set them free (as only a Scientologist can) they would go berserk, cry up their private police and generally cause unpleasantness. Indeed, one did—he was later assassinated by no desire of ours but because of the incompetence of his own fellows about him. He could have used Scientology. Instead, he promptly tried

---

1. **censorious:** severely critical; faultfinding.
2. **demented:** mentally deranged; insane; mad.

to shoot it down by ordering raids and various berserk actions on Scientology organizations. That he was then shot had nothing to do with us—but only demonstrated how incompetent and how mortal he really was.

As we become stronger, we can be completely openhanded with our help. Until we do, we can at least understand the one fact that greatness does not stem from savage wars or being known. It stems from being true to one's own decency, from going on helping others whatever they do or think or say and despite all savage acts against one; to persevere without changing one's basic attitude toward man.

A fully *trained* Scientologist is in a far better position to understand than a partly trained one. For the Scientologist who really knows is able not only to retain confidence in himself and what he can do, but also can understand why others do what they do. And so knowing, does not become baffled or dismayed by small defeats. To that degree, true greatness depends on total wisdom. They act as they do because they are what they are—trapped beings, crushed beneath an intolerable burden. And if they have gone mad for it and command the devastation of whole nations in errors of explanation, still one can understand why and can understand as well the extent of their madness. Why should one change and begin to hate just because others have lost themselves and their own destinies are too cruel for them to face?

Justice, mercy, forgiveness, all are unimportant beside

the ability not to change because of provocation or demands to do so.

One must act, one must preserve order and decency, but one need not hate or seek vengeance.

It is true that beings are frail and commit wrongs. Man is basically good but can act badly.

He only acts badly when his acts done for order and the safety of others are done with hatred. Or when his disciplines are founded only upon safety for himself regardless of all others; or worse, when he acts only out of a taste for cruelty.

To preserve no order at all is an insane act. One need only look at the possessions and environment of the insane to realize this. The able keep good order.

When cruelty in the name of discipline dominates a race, that race has been taught to hate. And that race is doomed.

The real lesson is to learn to love.

He who would walk scatheless through his days must learn this.

Never use what is done to one as a basis for hatred. Never desire revenge.

It requires real strength to love man. And to love him despite all invitations to do otherwise, all provocations and all reasons why one should not.

Happiness and strength endure only in the absence of hate. To hate alone is the road to disaster. To love is the road to strength. To love in spite of all is the secret of greatness. And may very well be the greatest secret in this universe.

*

YOU ASK

THIS BOOK ANSWERS!

You can search the *Encyclopaedia Britannica* from astronomy to the zodiac and still you won't find the answers you are looking for. That's where this book is different. You ask. It answers. It's called *What Is Scientology?*

You've already found truth in *Scientology*. About living, about you.

Now it's time for the full picture. Scientology is a vast subject and that's why we compiled this book. To show you that there's a gradient approach to complete knowledge of self and spiritual freedom. It'll show you how to get started.

You'll see the scope of Scientology in the world, learn what it means to be a *Scientologist*™ and what it is that makes Scientology a way of life.

This book answers **all** your questions.

864 pages, hardcover, packed with information, photos, illustrations, graphs and more.

- What the spirit, mind and body are.
- The life of its founder L. Ron Hubbard.
- The background and origins of Scientology.
- Programs for literacy, education, drug rehab, criminal reform all salvaging a world gone mad.
- Scientology* principles and application.
- What auditing is.
- A complete description of **all** the services in Scientology.
- Stories from those who know and use Scientology every day.

Get *What Is Scientology?*
It's your reference for life.

Order now. Call 1-800-334-5433

How did he uncover the truth about how the mind works?
LET L. RON HUBBARD TELL YOU HIMSELF

Ron explains how *Dianetics®* and Scientology came about, from the beginnings of his quest for truth— starting at the age of 12.

You'll travel with Ron through his years in Asia studying with mystics; at George Washington University where he discovered to his amazement that no one actually knew how the mind worked; in Hollywood, where he made his breakthrough discovery of the common denominator of all life; in World War II, where his experiments would prove that *function monitors structure,* or as he said, "thought was boss"; his achievement by 1947 of Clearing; his landmark publication of *Dianetics* in 1950; and beyond.

You'll hear how every step of his journey made him more determined to find the truth about the human mind and life—and how he *found* that truth.

Audio cassette. 60 minutes.

Order
THE STORY OF DIANETICS AND SCIENTOLOGY
Call 1-800-334-5433

Find out about our further list of individual lectures from the *Personal Achievement Series* by L. Ron Hubbard

You don't have to wait 'til the second coming to find the answers to life.

(Especially when they're already here.)

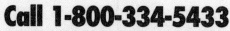

Call 1-800-334-5433

for your **free** catalog of L. Ron Hubbard's books and cassettes and find <u>the</u> answers you've been searching for.

GLOSSARY

aberration: a departure from rational thought or behavior. It means basically to err, to make mistakes, or more specifically to have fixed ideas which are not true. The word is also used in its scientific sense. It means departure from a straight line. If a line should go from A to B, then if it is *aberrated* it would go from A to some other point, to some other point, to some other point, to some other point, to some other point, and finally arrive at B. Taken in its scientific sense, it would also mean the lack of straightness or to see crookedly as, for example, a man sees a horse but thinks he sees an elephant. Aberrated conduct would be wrong conduct, or conduct not supported by reason. Aberration is opposed to sanity, which would be its opposite. From the Latin, *aberrare*, to wander from; Latin, *ab*, away, *errare*, to wander.

acceptance level: the degree of a person's willingness to accept people or things freely, monitored and determined by his consideration of the state or condition that those people or things must be in for him to be able to do so.

account, calling to: blaming; reprimanding.

accrue: accumulate, as by natural growth.

Adlerianism: referring to the theory of Alfred Adler

(1870–1937), an Austrian psychiatrist and psychologist. This theory stated in part that behavior is determined by compensation for feelings of inferiority.

aggregation: the collecting of separate things into one mass or whole.

air, up in the: not settled; not decided.

alloyed: weakened or spoiled by adding something that reduces value or pleasure.

alter ego: *(psychoanalysis)* another aspect of oneself.

amperes: the standard units for measuring the strength of an electric current.

apathy: a complete withdrawal from person or people. There is no real attempt to contact oneself and no attempt to contact others. A very docile and obedient, if sick, state of not-beingness. It is near death or an imitation of death. For example, a person in apathy would say, "What's the use? All is lost."

ARC triangle: a triangle which is a symbol of the fact that affinity, reality and communication act together as a whole entity and that one of them cannot be considered unless the other two are also taken into account. Without affinity there is no reality or communication. Without reality or some agreement, affinity and communication are absent.

Without communication there can be no affinity or reality. It is only necessary to improve one corner of this very valuable triangle in Scientology in order to improve the remaining two corners.

auditing: the application of Dianetics or Scientology processes and procedures to someone by a trained auditor. The exact definition of auditing is: The action of asking a person a question (which he can understand and answer), getting an answer to that question and acknowledging him for that answer. Also called *processing*.

auditor: a person trained and qualified in applying Dianetics and/or Scientology processes and procedures to individuals for their betterment; called an auditor because *auditor* means *one who listens*.

Babylon: the capital of an ancient empire called Babylonia which was located in southwest Asia and flourished from 2100 to 538 B.C.

badlands: any section of barren land where rapid erosion has cut the loose, dry soil or soft rocks into strange shapes.

Bedlam: an old insane asylum (in full, St. Mary of Bethlehem) in London, infamous for the brutal ill-treatment inflicted upon the insane.

beingness: the assumption or choosing of a category of identity. Beingness is assumed by oneself or given to oneself or is attained. Examples of beingness would be one's own name, one's profession, one's physical characteristics, one's role in a game—each and all of these could be called one's beingness.

bench, on a: presiding in a law court; serving as a judge.

blows off: suddenly dissipates (disperses; vanishes).

British broadcasting company: reference to the *British Broadcasting Corporation*, the government-sponsored radio and television company of the United Kingdom. Often abbreviated as *BBC*.

British thermal unit: the quantity of heat required to raise the temperature of one pound of water one degree Fahrenheit.

cartel: a large group of business firms that agree to operate as a monopoly, especially to regulate prices and production.

cataclysmic: characterized by violent changes; calamities.

catch (someone or something) out: catch or discover (someone or something) in deceit or in error.

cause-point: the originator of something; the point from which something was begun or dreamed up.

caving in: giving in; yielding; submitting.

censor: *(psychoanalysis)* in early Freudian dream therapy this was considered to be the force which repressed ideas, impulses and feelings and prevented them from entering consciousness in their original, undisguised forms.

censorious: severely critical; faultfinding.

Chaldea: province of Babylonia, the ancient empire in what is now southern Iraq. *See also* **Babylon** in this glossary.

charge: harmful energy or force accumulated and stored within the reactive mind, resulting from the conflicts and unpleasant experiences that a person has had. *See also* **reactive** in this glossary.

Christian Science: a church founded by Mary Baker Eddy (1821–1910), American religious leader, editor and author.

classic: serving as a standard, model or guide.

Clear: the name of a state achieved through auditing or an individual who has achieved this state. A Clear is a being who no longer has his own reactive mind. A Clear is an unaberrated person and is rational in that he forms the best possible solutions he can on the data he has and from his viewpoint. The Clear has no engrams which can be restimulated to throw out the correctness of computation by entering hidden and false data.

collusion: secret agreement for fraudulent or illegal purposes; conspiracy.

colonial: of or pertaining to a group of the same kind (of animals, plants or one-celled organisms) living or growing together.

communication line: the route along which a communication travels from one person to another; the line on which particles flow; any sequences through which a message of any character may go.

confront: face without flinching or avoiding. *Confront* is actually the ability to be there comfortably and perceive.

conjugations: systematic arrangements of the forms of a verb.

contravenes: goes against; opposes; conflicts with; violates.

cooked-up: made-up; invented.

counter-effort: effort is divided into the effort of the individual himself and the efforts of the environment (physical) against the individual. The individual's own effort is simply called effort. The efforts of the environment are called counter-efforts.

criteria: standards, rules or tests by which things can be judged.

cuffed: struck; beat.

culture: a growth of bacteria or other microorganisms in a specially prepared nourishing substance.

dark operations: evil, wicked or harmful activities. Also known as *black operations*.

dearth: scarcity or lack.

debased: lowered in value, quality, character, dignity.

demented: mentally deranged; insane; mad.

demonology: the study of demons or of beliefs about them.

Dianetics: comes from the Greek words *dia*, meaning "through" and *nous*, meaning "soul." Dianetics is a methodology developed by L. Ron Hubbard which can help alleviate such things as unwanted sensations and emotions, irrational fears and psychosomatic illnesses. It is most accurately described as *what the soul is doing to the body through the mind*.

dickens with it: I don't care about it. *Dickens* is a word used instead of *devil* or *hell*.

differentiation: the ability to "tell the difference" between one person and another, one object and another. It indicates a person is sane. As soon as he begins to confuse his wife with his mother or his coat with his father's coat, he is on the road toward insanity.

Diogenes: (412?–323 B.C.) Greek philosopher. According to tradition, he once went through the streets holding up a lantern, "looking for an honest man."

disabused: *(in normal usage)* freed from false ideas; put right. Used here in the sense "robbed or deprived of."

down scale: down the Tone Scale; into a state of decreased awareness; into the lower-level emotions, such as apathy, anger, etc. *See also* **Tone Scale** in this glossary.

dramatized: acted out; demonstrated.

dwindling spiral: a phenomenon of ARC whereby when one breaks some affinity, a little bit of the reality goes down, and then communication goes down, which makes it impossible to get affinity as high as before; so a little bit more gets knocked off affinity, and then reality goes down, and then communication. This is the dwindling spiral in progress, until it hits the bottom—death—which is no affinity, no communication and no reality.

dynamic(s): there could be said to be eight urges (drives, impulses) in life. These we call dynamics. These are motives or motivations. We call them the eight dynamics. These are urges for survival as or through (1) self, (2) sex and family, (3) groups, (4) all mankind, (5) living things (plants and animals), (6) the material universe, (7) spirits and (8) infinity or the Supreme Being.

ebb: decline or decay.

effect-point: the receipt-point of an idea, particle or mass.

ego: *(psychoanalysis)* that part of the psyche (soul) which experiences the external world through the senses, organizes the thought processes rationally and governs action.

engineering: the science concerned with putting scientific knowledge to practical uses, divided into different branches, as civil, electrical, mechanical or chemical engineering.

engram: a mental image picture which is a recording of a time of physical pain and unconsciousness. It must by definition have impact or injury as part of its contents.

enigma: a perplexing, baffling or seemingly unexplainable matter, person, etc.

Ennead of Heliopolis: the group of nine gods *(Ennead)* of ancient Egyptian religion originating from the city of Heliopolis, one of the principal religious centers of the period.

enturbulated: made turbulent or agitated and disturbed.

equation: a condition involving some equivalence or relation.

esoteric: beyond the understanding or knowledge of most people.

essence, in the final: essentially; at bottom, often despite appearances.

estate: social status or rank.

ethics: rationality toward the highest level of survival for the individual, the future race, the group and mankind. Ethics is reason and the contemplation of optimum survival.

facile: able to move, act, work, proceed, etc., with ease.

fancy: the power to imagine; imagination.

fight shy: keep away from; avoid.

fission: the act of cleaving or splitting into parts. *Nuclear fission* is the splitting of the nucleus of an atom into nuclei of lighter atoms, accompanied by the release of energy. The word comes from Latin *fission,* meaning "a splitting, dividing."

flattens: carries on with (a process or question) until the question no longer produces a reaction.

flight: *(figurative)* the act or fact of soaring above or beyond what is ordinary.

flotsam and jetsam: transient, unemployed people.

flows: progresses of energy between two points.

foregone conclusion: a safe assumption about some future event.

franchises: the privileges or rights granted by a government.

frequency: the number of times something is repeated in a certain period (i.e., a *frequency* of 1,000 vibrations per second).

Freud: Sigmund Freud (1856–1939), Austrian physician and the founder of psychoanalysis. *See also* **psychoanalysis** in this glossary.

Galen: (c. A.D. 130–200) Greek physician. A prolific writer, his works were for centuries the standards for anatomy and physiology.

game: a contest of person against person or team against team. A game consists of freedoms, barriers and purposes. It also consists of control and uncontrol. An opponent in a game must be an uncontrolled factor, otherwise one would know exactly where the game was going and how it would end and it would not be a game at all.

game-conservation: the official protection and care of wild animals, birds and fish which are hunted or caught for sport or for food.

generation: the act or process of bringing into being; origination; production.

genetic line: the protoplasm (essential living matter of cells) line. It consists of the total of incidents which have occurred during the evolution of the body itself.

ghouls: *(Oriental folklore)* evil spirits that rob graves and feed on the flesh of the dead.

grade: a series of processes which are run on a person with the purpose of bringing him to a particular state of release (what occurs when a person separates from his reactive mind or some part of it).

gradient scale: a scale of condition graduated from zero to infinity. On a scale of certainty, everything above zero or center would be more and more certain, approaching an infinite certainty, and everything below zero or center would be more and more uncertain, approaching an infinite uncertainty. Absolutes are considered to be unobtainable.

habituated: made used to; accustomed; familiarized with.

hand, at every: on all sides; in every direction.

Harvey: William Harvey (1578–1657), English physician and discoverer of the mechanics of blood circulation.

herculean: having enormous strength, courage or size.

high-toned beings: individuals who are high on the Tone Scale. They think wholly into the future. They are extroverted toward their environment. They clearly observe the environment with full perception unclouded by undistinguished fears about the environment. They think very little about themselves but operate automatically in their own interests. They enjoy existence. Their calculations are swift and accurate. They are very self-confident. They *know* they know and do not even bother to assert that they know. They control their environment. *See also* **Tone Scale** in this glossary.

humanities: the branches of learning concerned with human thought and relations, as distinguished from the sciences; especially literature, philosophy, history, etc.

humbugs: persons who are not what they claim to be; impostors.

hypochondria: *(psychiatry)* an excessive preoccupation with one's health, usually focused on some particular symptom.

id: *(psychoanalysis)* the division of the psyche (soul) associated with instinctual impulses and demands for immediate satisfaction of primitive needs.

identification: the inability to evaluate differences in time, location, form, composition or importance.

ideology: the doctrines, opinions or way of thinking of an individual, class, etc.; specifically, the ideas on which a political, economic or social system is based.

implanter: one who administers an *implant,* an enforced command or series of commands installed in the reactive mind below the awareness level of the individual to cause him to react or behave in a prearranged way without his "knowing it."

individuation: a withdrawal out of groups and into only self. The mechanics of individuation are, first, communication into and, then, refusal to communicate into.

inkblots: any of a group of irregular patterns made by blots of ink and used in psychological testing.

inorganic: not containing organic matter. Chemical compounds without hydrocarbons (hydrogen and carbon) are usually inorganic.

instilled: pervaded or inspired (with opinions, feelings, habits, etc.).

interminably: without, or apparently without, end; endlessly.

invalidate: refute or degrade or discredit or deny.

IQ: *I*ntelligence *Q*uotient: a number intended to indicate a person's level of intelligence. Intelligence quotient (IQ) ratings are a measure of an individual's capacity for learning something new; they are a scale based upon how old in years a person has become compared to how "old" he is mentally.

iron steed: *(figurative)* a motorcycle.

irreligion: an indifference or hostility to religion.

Job: the central character in the Book of Job, an ancient Indian work, later incorporated into the Bible. In this story, Job endures much suffering but does not lose his faith in God.

Joe Miller joke book: a book of old or worn-out jokes, erroneously attributed to Joe Miller (1684–1738), an English actor and comedian. The book was actually published a year after his death and went through many printings. Timeworn jests are sometimes called "a Joe Miller."

Jungianism: referring to the theories of Carl Gustav Jung (1875–1961), Swiss psychologist and psychiatrist. These include in part a theory of the unconscious and the theory of two attitude types (extroversion and introversion).

jurisprudence: a system or body of law; a legal system.

keel: the chief timber or steel piece extending along the entire length of the bottom of a boat or ship and supporting the frame: it sometimes protrudes beneath the hull.

Kraepelin: Emil Kraepelin (1856–1926), German psychiatrist. Developed a system of psychiatric classification.

legislation: law or laws made by legislatures for countries or states.

legislatures: bodies of persons given the responsibility and power to make laws for countries or states.

Lenin: Vladimir I. Lenin (1870–1924), Russian communist leader. He was an agitator for socialism. During World War I he urged socialists in all countries to rise against their own governments, and he assumed leadership of the Russian Revolution in 1917.

Leonardo da Vinci: (1452–1519) Italian painter, sculptor, architect, engineer and scientist.

liquid fire: flaming petroleum or the like, as employed against an enemy in warfare.

livingness: the activity of going along a certain course, impelled (driven) by a purpose and with some place to arrive.

lobbying: influencing lawmakers in voting for or against certain laws, in order to benefit a special group.

longbow: a large bow drawn by hand and shooting a long, feathered arrow.

love nests: dwellings of lovers, especially places where illicit (not allowed by law, custom, rule, etc.) lovers live or meet.

low-toned mockery: a little band down very close to death on the Tone Scale. Anything that is in that band is a mockery of anything higher. Some fellow dresses in a very good way and a comedian comes out on the stage, dressed overdone with the same characteristics. That would be a lower-scale mockery of a person dressing well. *See also* **Tone Scale** in this glossary.

Lucifer: the chief rebel angel who was cast out of heaven; Satan; the Devil.

Luzon: main island of the Philippines.

malefactor: an evildoer or criminal.

maltension: *mal-* is a prefix meaning "bad or badly, wrong, ill." *Tension* means "a balancing of forces or elements in opposition." Therefore, *maltension* is bad or wrong balance of forces.

Maxwell, James Clerk: (1831–1879) Scottish physicist whose research and discoveries advanced the knowledge of electromagnetism, color perception and other areas.

medico: a physician or surgeon; doctor.

men from Mars: referring to a radio dramatization by Orson Welles (in 1938) of H.G. Wells' *War of the Worlds*. It was done in the form of a newscast and caused a panic when people thought that the Martians had actually invaded the Earth. *See also* **Welles, Orson** and **Wells, H.G.** in this glossary.

mental image pictures: copies of the physical universe as it goes by; we call a mental image picture a facsimile when it is a "photograph" of the physical universe sometime in the past. We call a mental image picture a mock-up when it is created by the thetan or for the thetan and does not consist of photographs of the physical universe. We call a mental image picture a hallucination, or more properly an automaticity (something uncontrolled), when it is created by another and seen by self.

meteorologist: a person who studies meteorology, the science dealing with the atmosphere and its phenomena, including weather and climate.

militarist: a person who supports or advocates the policy of maintaining a large military establishment.

millennia: periods of one thousand years.

misemotion: a coined word used in Dianetics and Scientology to mean an emotion or emotional reaction that is inappropriate to the present time situation. It is taken from *mis-* (wrong) + *emotion*. To say that a person was *misemotional* would indicate that the person did not display the emotion called for by the actual circumstances of the situation. Being misemotional would be synonymous with being irrational. One can fairly judge the rationality of any individual by the correctness of the emotion he displays in a given set of circumstances. To be joyful and happy when circumstances call for joy and happiness would be rational. To display grief without sufficient present time cause would be irrational.

mock (it) up: create it. In Scientology the word *mock-up* is used to mean, in essence, something which a person makes up himself. The term was derived from the World War II phrase for miniature models that were constructed to symbolize weapons (airplanes, ships, artillery, etc.) or areas of attack (hills, rivers, buildings, etc.) for use in planning a battle.

montage: any combination of disparate (different in kind) elements that forms or is felt to form a unified, whole, single image, etc.

morals: a code of good conduct laid down out of the experience of the race to serve as a uniform yardstick for the conduct of individuals and groups.

Morse code: a system by which letters, numbers, punctuation and other signs are expressed by dots, dashes and spaces or by wigwags of a flag, long and short sounds or flashes of light. Morse code is now used mainly in signaling and in some telegraphy.

mystic: a person who practices mysticism, the beliefs or practices of those who claim to have experiences based on intuition, meditation, etc., of a spiritual nature, by which they learn truths not known by ordinary people.

nay: not only that, but also.

network: any system of lines or channels interlacing or crossing like the fabric of a net; also used figuratively, as, for example, a network of falsehoods.

neurosis: an emotional state containing conflicts and emotional data inhibiting the abilities or welfare of the individual.

neurosurgery: surgery of the brain or other nerve tissue.

neurotic: characterizing one who is insane or disturbed on some subject (as opposed to a psychotic person, who is just insane in general).

nomenclature: the set of terms used to describe things in a particular subject.

nuclear physics: that branch of physics (the science of relationships between matter and energy) which deals with atoms, their nuclear structure, and the behavior of nuclear particles.

old-school: (of or like) a group of people who cling to traditional or conservative ideas, methods, etc.

organic: *(chemistry)* of or having to do with compounds containing carbon.

Osiris: one of the chief gods of ancient Egypt, ruler of the lower world and judge of the dead. He represented good and productivity and is identified with the Nile.

overwrought: extremely or excessively excited or agitated.

para-Scientology: a category of data in Scientology which includes all greater or lesser uncertainties and questionable things; things in Scientology of which the common, normal observer cannot be sure with a little study.

parity: equality, as in amount, status, character.

parliaments: highest lawmaking bodies in some countries.

passenger pigeons: long-tailed American pigeons, noted for their extended migratory flights, but extinct since 1914. Passenger pigeons are believed to have lived in greater numbers than any other vertebrate (having a backbone) land animal of which records exist, but were repeatedly slaughtered in the 1800s for US food markets during the height of their breeding season.

pause, be given: be made hesitant or unsure, as from surprise or doubt.

Pavlov: Ivan Petrovich Pavlov (1849–1936), Russian physiologist; noted for behavioral experiments on dogs.

pestiferous: annoying; bothersome.

phoneticized: represented or spelled as they would sound when spoken, using symbols to show pronunciation.

physical universe: the universe of matter, energy, space and time. It would be the universe of the planets, their rocks, rivers and oceans, the universe of stars and galaxies, the universe of burning suns and time.

physics: the science which deals with relationships between matter and energy, including subjects such as mechanics, heat, light, sound, electricity, magnetism, radiation and atomic structure.

Picasso: Pablo Picasso (1881–1973), Spanish painter and sculptor. Known as one of the foremost twentieth-century artists.

pose: attitude or frame of mind.

postulate: a conclusion, decision or resolution made by the individual himself.

pots: (*British slang*) persons of importance.

pounds: the basic unit of money in the United Kingdom; also called *pounds sterling*.

preempt: take over.

prefrontal-lobotomied: subjected to a prefrontal lobotomy, a surgical procedure in which the frontal lobes are separated from the rest of the brain by cutting the connecting nerve fibers. Used by psychiatry supposedly for the purpose of relieving symptoms of mental illness.

preponderance: superiority in weight, power, influence, numbers, etc.

presumptuous: too bold or forward; taking too much for granted.

prime: primary, original, fundamental; from which others are derived or on which they depend.

Prime Mover Unmoved: a concept originating with the Greek philosopher Aristotle. It means the first cause of all movement, itself immovable.

primordial: pertaining to or existing at or from the very beginning.

process: a set of questions asked or commands given by a Scientology or Dianetics practitioner to help a person find out things about himself or life and to improve his condition.

processing: the application of Dianetics and/or Scientology processes and procedures to individuals for their betterment. The exact definition of processing is: The action of asking a person a question (which he can understand and answer), getting an answer to that question and acknowledging him for that answer. Also called *auditing*. *See also* **process** in this glossary.

protoplasm line: *see* **genetic line** in this glossary.

psychoanalysis: a system of mental therapy developed in 1894 by Sigmund Freud. It depended upon the following practices for its effects: The patient was made to talk about and recall his childhood for years while the practitioner brought about a transfer of the patient's personality to his own and searched for hidden sexual incidents believed by Freud to be the only cause of aberration. The practitioner read sexual significances into all statements and evaluated them for the patient along sexual lines. Each of these points later proved to be based upon false premises and incomplete research, accounting for their lack of result and the subsequent failure of the subject and its offshoots. *See also* **Freud** in this glossary.

psychology: the study of the human brain and stimulus-response mechanisms. Its code word was: "Man, to be happy, must adjust to his environment." In other words, man, to be happy, must be a total effect.

psychosis: any severe form of mental disorder; insanity.

psychosomatic: *psycho* refers to mind and *somatic* refers to body; the term *psychosomatic* means the mind making the body ill or illnesses which have been created physically within the body by derangement of the mind.

psychotic: characterizing a person who is physically or mentally harmful to those about him out of proportion to the amount of use he is to them.

"quality of mercy is not strained . . . , The": the beginning line of a passage from act four, scene one of Shakespeare's play *The Merchant of Venice* (1596–1597). *See also* **Shakespeare** in this glossary.

randomity: a consideration of motion. There is plus randomity and minus randomity. There can be, from the individual's consideration, too much or too little motion, or enough motion. "Enough motion" is measured by the consideration of the individual.

rationalize: justify; make excuses to explain irrational behavior.

reactive: irrational, reacting instead of acting; thinkingness or behavior dictated by the reactive mind rather than the individual's own present time determinism. *See also* **reactive mind** in this glossary.

reactive mind: that portion of a person's mind which works on a totally stimulus-response basis, which is not under his volitional control and which

exerts force and power of command over his awareness, purposes, thoughts, body and actions.

rear guard: a part of an army or military force
detached from the main body to bring up and
guard the rear from surprise attack, especially in a
retreat. Used figuratively.

recriminations: counteraccusations; accusations
brought in turn by the accused against the accuser.

redwood: an evergreen tree of the California and
southern Oregon coasts. It is amongst the world's
largest trees, reaching a height of over 300 feet and
an age of several thousand years.

repress: keep under control, check or suppress
(desires, feelings, actions, tears, etc.).

restimulation: reactivation of a past memory due to
similar circumstances in the present approximating
circumstances of the past.

rights, put to: put into good or proper condition or
order.

Rockefeller: of or having to do with the Rockefeller
family or its international financial interests.
Originally founded in the oil business by John D.
Rockefeller (1839–1937), his heirs have continued
to expand its influence in many areas internationally.

rompers: a loose outer garment, usually consisting of short bloomers and top, worn by young children at play.

rows: noisy quarrels, disputes or disturbances; squabbles, brawls or commotions.

run: the typical, ordinary or average kind.

sanguinely: in a cheerfully optimistic, hopeful or confident manner.

schizophrenics: persons suffering from schizophrenia, a mental illness in which an individual is being two people madly inside of himself. It is a psychiatry classification derived from the Latin *schizo*, meaning "split," and the Greek *phren*, meaning "mind."

Scientology: comes from the Latin *scio*, which means "know" and the Greek word *logos*, meaning "the word or outward form by which the inward thought is expressed and made known." Thus, Scientology means knowing about knowing. Scientology is an applied religious philosophy developed by L. Ron Hubbard. It is the study and handling of the spirit in relationship to itself, universes and other life.

self-abnegation: lack of consideration for oneself or one's own interest; self-denial.

self-determinism: power of choice; power of decision; ability to decide or determine the course of one's actions.

semaphore: a system of signaling by the use of two flags, one held in each hand: the letters of the alphabet are represented by the various positions of the arms.

sequitur: *(Latin)* that which follows as a consequence; that which follows logically.

Shakespeare: William Shakespeare (1564–1616), English poet and dramatist of the Elizabethan period (1558–1603), the most widely known author in all English literature.

skid row: a slum street or section full of cheap saloons, rooming houses, etc., frequented by derelicts (penniless persons who are homeless and jobless).

slant: viewpoint; opinion; attitude.

socialization: the action of training (an individual) for society or a social environment.

spontaneous combustion: the process of catching fire as a result of heat generated by internal chemical action. Used satirically in this book to describe *spontaneous generation*, the theory, now discredited, that living organisms can originate in nonliving matter independently of other living matter.

Stalingrad: former name of Volgograd, a city on the Volga River in the country of Russia. Stalingrad was the site of a crucial battle against the invading German army in World War II (Aug. 1942 to Feb.

1943). Although the city was practically destroyed, Russia's defense finally forced the Germans to retreat and then surrender. The battle was the turning point in Germany's military power in the war and is considered one of the great turning points in military history.

stimulus-response: of or having to do with a certain stimulus automatically giving a certain response.

subconscious: *see* **unconscious mind** in this glossary.

subordinate: make obedient or submissive (to); control; subdue.

sweetness and light: persons or things exhibiting unusual tolerance, understanding or sympathy (often used ironically when such a display is entirely out of character).

sympathetic: (1) in agreement; harmonious; in accord. (2) *(physics)* noting or pertaining to vibrations, sounds, etc., produced by a body as the direct result of similar vibrations in a different body.

taxidermist: one who practices the art of preparing, stuffing and mounting the skins of animals, especially so as to make them appear lifelike.

technology: the methods of application of an art or science as opposed to mere knowledge of the science or art itself.

techno-space society: a society with technology advanced to the level of being capable of space travel.

tenement: a rundown and often overcrowded apartment house, especially in a poor section of a large city.

tenets: principles, doctrines or beliefs held as truths, as by some group.

tenuous: weak; flimsy.

thetan: the person himself—not his body or his name, the physical universe, his mind or anything else; that which is aware of being aware; the identity which is the individual. The term was coined to eliminate any possible confusion with older, invalid concepts. It comes from the Greek letter theta (θ), which the Greeks used to represent *thought* or perhaps *spirit*, to which an *n* is added to make a noun in the modern style used to create words in engineering. It is also θ^n or "theta to the nth degree," meaning unlimited or vast.

time track: the consecutive record of mental image pictures which accumulate through a person's life or lives. It is very exactly dated. The time track is the entire sequence of "now" incidents, complete with all sense messages, picked up by a person during his whole existence.

tirade: a long, vehement speech.

Tone Scale: a scale, in Scientology, which shows the emotional tones of a person. These, ranged from the highest to the lowest, are, in part, serenity, enthusiasm (as we proceed downward), conservatism, boredom, antagonism, anger, covert hostility, fear, grief, apathy. An arbitrary numerical value is given to each level on the scale. There are many aspects of the *Tone Scale* and using it makes possible the prediction of human behavior. For further information on the *Tone Scale,* read the book *Self Analysis* by L. Ron Hubbard.

tooth-and-claw: characterized by the need of fighting *tooth and claw,* that is, fighting with great determination and effort (against someone or something).

track: *see* **time track** in this glossary.

travail: intense pain; agony.

typhoid: an infectious, often fatal, febrile (feverish) disease characterized by intestinal inflammation and ulceration, caused by the typhoid bacillus, which is usually introduced with food or drink.

unconscious mind: a term from psychoanalysis. It is said to be the sum of all thoughts, memories, impulses, desires, feelings, etc., of which the individual is not conscious but which influence his emotions and behavior. In actuality, the "unconscious" is the sum of all a man's bad experiences and nothing more mysterious than that. In Dianetics and Scientology it is called the reactive mind. *See also* **reactive** and **reactive mind** in this glossary.

vectors: physical quantities with both magnitude and direction, such as a force or velocity.

vivisection: medical research consisting of surgical operations or other experiments performed on living animals to study the structure and function of living organs and parts, and to investigate the effects of diseases and therapy.

watts: units of electrical power.

Welles, Orson: (1915–1985) American actor, director and producer. Produced a radio dramatization in 1938 of H.G. Wells' *The War of the Worlds*. It was done in the form of a news broadcast and caused widespread panic in the US at the time when people thought that the Martians had actually invaded the Earth. *See also* **men from Mars** and **Wells, H.G.** in this glossary.

well grounded: having a thorough basic knowledge of.

Wells, H.G.: Herbert George Wells (1866–1946), English novelist and journalist. Wells is known for his science fiction, his satirical novels and his popularized accounts of history and science. The first great writer of science fiction, H.G. Wells is author of *The Time Machine, The War of the Worlds* and others.

wog: *(Scientology slang)* a common, ordinary, run-of-the-mill, garden-variety humanoid, by which we mean an individual that considers that he is a body and does not know that he is there as a spirit at all.

word of mouth: informal oral communication.

wreak: inflict; cause.

yeast: the substance that causes dough for most kinds of bread to rise and that causes beer to ferment. Yeast consists of very small, single-celled plants that grow quickly in a liquid containing sugar.

INDEX

CHURCHES OF SCIENTOLOGY
AROUND THE WORLD

Churches of Scientology exist on all continents around the globe. If you would like more information about Dianetics or Scientology, contact the organization nearest you or call 1-800-334-5433.

USA

Albuquerque
Church of Scientology
8106 Menaul Blvd. N.E.
Albuquerque, New Mexico 87110

Ann Arbor
Church of Scientology
2355 West Stadium Blvd.
Ann Arbor, Michigan 48103

Atlanta
Church of Scientology
1132 West Peachtree Street
Atlanta, Georgia 30324

Austin
Church of Scientology
2200 Guadalupe
Austin, Texas 78705

Boston
Church of Scientology
448 Beacon Street
Boston, Massachusetts 02115

Buffalo
Church of Scientology
47 West Huron Street
Buffalo, New York 14202

Chicago
Church of Scientology
3009 North Lincoln Avenue
Chicago, Illinois 60657

Cincinnati
Church of Scientology
215 West 4th Street, 5th Floor
Cincinnati, Ohio 45202

Clearwater
Church of Scientology
Flag Service Organization
210 South Fort Harrison Avenue
Clearwater, Florida 34616

Church of Scientology
Flag Ship Service Organization
c/o *Freewinds* Relay Office
118 N. Fort Harrison Avenue
Clearwater, Florida 34615

Columbus
Church of Scientology
30 North High Street
Columbus, Ohio 43215

Dallas
Church of Scientology
Celebrity Centre Dallas
10500 Steppington Drive, Suite 100
Dallas, Texas 75230

Denver
Church of Scientology
3385 S. Bannock
Englewood, Colorado 80110

Detroit
Church of Scientology
321 Williams Street
Royal Oak, Michigan 48067

Honolulu
Church of Scientology
1148 Bethel Street
Honolulu, Hawaii 96813

Kansas City
Church of Scientology
3619 Broadway
Kansas City, Missouri 64111

Las Vegas
Church of Scientology
846 East Sahara Avenue
Las Vegas, Nevada 89104

Church of Scientology
Celebrity Centre Las Vegas
1100 South 10th Street
Las Vegas, Nevada 89104

Long Island
Church of Scientology
99 Railroad Station Plaza
Hicksville, New York 11801

Los Angeles and vicinity
Church of Scientology
4810 Sunset Boulevard
Los Angeles, California 90027

Church of Scientology
1451 Irvine Boulevard
Tustin, California 92680

Church of Scientology
1277 East Colorado Boulevard
Pasadena, California 91106

Church of Scientology
3619 West Magnolia Boulevard
Burbank, California 91506

Church of Scientology
American Saint Hill Organization
1413 L. Ron Hubbard Way
Los Angeles, California 90027

Church of Scientology
American Saint Hill Foundation
1413 L. Ron Hubbard Way
Los Angeles, California 90027

Church of Scientology
Advanced Organization of
  Los Angeles
1306 L. Ron Hubbard Way
Los Angeles, California 90027

Church of Scientology
Celebrity Centre International
5930 Franklin Avenue
Hollywood, California 90028

Los Gatos
Church of Scientology
475 Alberto Way, Suite 110
Los Gatos, California 95032

Miami
Church of Scientology
120 Giralda Avenue
Coral Gables, Florida 33134

Minneapolis
Church of Scientology
Twin Cities
1011 Nicollet Mall
Minneapolis, Minnesota 55403

Mountain View
Church of Scientology
2483 Old Middlefield Way
Mountain View, California 96043

Nashville
Church of Scientology
Celebrity Centre Nashville
1503 16th Ave. So.
Nashville, Tennessee 37212

New Haven
Church of Scientology
909 Whalley Avenue
New Haven, Connecticut 06515

New York City
Church of Scientology
227 West 46th Street
New York City, New York 10036

Church of Scientology
Celebrity Centre New York
65 East 82nd Street
New York City, New York 10028

Orlando
Church of Scientology
1830 East Colonial Drive
Orlando, Florida 32803

Philadelphia
Church of Scientology
1315 Race Street
Philadelphia, Pennsylvania 19107

Phoenix
Church of Scientology
2111 W. University Dr.
Mesa, Arizona 85201

Portland
Church of Scientology
323 S.W. Washington
Portland, Oregon 97204

Church of Scientology
Celebrity Centre Portland
709 Southwest Salmon Street
Portland, Oregon 97205

Sacramento
Church of Scientology
825 15th Street
Sacramento, California 95814

Salt Lake City
Church of Scientology
1931 S. 1100 East
Salt Lake City, Utah 84106

San Diego
Church of Scientology
1330 4th Ave.
San Diego, California 92101

San Francisco
Church of Scientology
83 McAllister Street
San Francisco, California 94102

San Jose
Church of Scientology
80 E. Rosemary
San Jose, California 95112

Santa Barbara
Church of Scientology
524 State Street
Santa Barbara, California 93101

Seattle
Church of Scientology
2226 3rd Avenue
Seattle, Washington 98121

St. Louis
Church of Scientology
9510 Page Boulevard
St. Louis, Missouri 63132

Tampa
Church of Scientology
3617 Henderson Blvd.
Tampa, Florida 33609

Washington, DC
Founding Church of Scientology
of Washington, DC
1701 20th Street N.W.
Washington, DC 20009

Puerto Rico

Hato Rey
Church of Scientology
272 JT Piniero Avenue
Hyde Park, Hato Rey
Puerto Rico 00918

Canada

Edmonton
Church of Scientology
10187 112th St.
Edmonton, Alberta
Canada T5K 1M1

Kitchener
Church of Scientology
104 King St. West
Kitchener, Ontario
Canada N2G 2K6

Montreal
Church of Scientology
4489 Papineau Street
Montréal, Québec
Canada H2H 1T7

Ottawa
Church of Scientology
150 Rideau Street, 2nd Floor
Ottawa, Ontario
Canada K1N 5X6

Quebec
Church of Scientology
350 Bd Chareste Est
Québec, Québec
Canada G1K 3H5

Toronto
Church of Scientology
696 Yonge Street, 2nd Floor
Toronto, Ontario
Canada M4Y 2A7

Vancouver
Church of Scientology
401 West Hasting Street
Vancouver, British Columbia
Canada V6B 1L5

Winnipeg
Church of Scientology
388 Donald Street, Suite 210
Winnipeg, Manitoba
Canada R3B 2J4

United Kingdom

Birmingham
Church of Scientology
Albert House, 3rd Floor
24 Albert Street
Birmingham, England B4 7UD

Brighton
Church of Scientology
5 St. Georges Place
London Road
Brighton, Sussex
England BN1 4GA

East Grinstead
Church of Scientology
Saint Hill Foundation
Saint Hill Manor
East Grinstead, West Sussex
England RH19 4JY

Advanced Organization Saint Hill
Saint Hill Manor
East Grinstead, West Sussex
England RH19 4JY

Edinburgh
Hubbard Academy of
  Personal Independence
20 Southbridge
Edinburgh, Scotland EH1 1LL

London
Church of Scientology
68 Tottenham Court Road
London, England W1P 0BB

Manchester
Church of Scientology
258 Deansgate
Manchester, England M3 4BG

Plymouth
Church of Scientology
41 Ebrington Street
Plymouth, Devon
England PL4 9AA

Sunderland
Church of Scientology
51 Fawcett Street
Sunderland, Tyne and Wear
England SR1 1RS

Austria

Vienna
Church of Scientology
Schottenfeldgasse 13/15
1070 Wien, Austria

Church of Scientology
Celebrity Centre Vienna
Senefeldergasse 11/5
1100 Wien, Austria

Belgium

Brussels
Church of Scientology
61, rue du Prince Royal
1050 Bruxelles, Belgium

Denmark

Aarhus
Church of Scientology
Vester Alle 26
8000 Aarhus C, Denmark

Copenhagen
Church of Scientology
Store Kongensgade 55
1264 Copenhagen K, Denmark

Church of Scientology
Gammel Kongevej 3–5, 1
1610 Copenhagen V, Denmark

Church of Scientology
Advanced Organization
  Saint Hill for Europe and Africa
Jernbanegade 6
1608 Copenhagen V, Denmark

France

Angers
Church of Scientology
21, rue Paul Bert
49100 Angers, France

Clermont-Ferrand
Church of Scientology
6, rue Dulaure
63000 Clermont-Ferrand, France

Lyon
Church of Scientology
3, place des Capucins
69001 Lyon, France

Paris
Church of Scientology
7, rue Jules César
75012 Paris, France

Church of Scientology
Celebrity Centre Paris
69, rue Legendre
75017 Paris, France

Saint-Étienne
Church of Scientology
24, rue Marengo
42000 Saint-Étienne, France

Germany

Berlin
Church of Scientology
Sponholzstraße 51–52
12159 Berlin, Germany

Düsseldorf
Church of Scientology
Friedrichstraße 28
40217 Düsseldorf, Germany

Church of Scientology
Celebrity Centre Düsseldorf
Luisenstraße 23
40215 Düsseldorf, Germany

Frankfurt
Church of Scientology
Darmstädter Landstraße 213
60598 Frankfurt, Germany

Hamburg
Church of Scientology
Steindamm 63
20099 Hamburg, Germany

Church of Scientology
Eppendorfer Landstraße 35
20249 Hamburg, Germany

Hanover
Church of Scientology
Hubertusstraße 2
30163 Hannover, Germany

Munich
Church of Scientology
Beichstraße 12
80802 München, Germany

Stuttgart
Church of Scientology
Hohenheimerstr. 9
70184 Stuttgart, Germany

Israel

Tel Aviv
College of Dianetics and Scientology
12 Shontzion
Tel Aviv 61573, Israel

Italy

Brescia
Church of Scientology
Via Fratelli Bronzetti, 20
25122 Brescia, Italy

Catania
Church of Scientology
Via Garibaldi, 9
95121 Catania, Italy

Milan
Church of Scientology
Via Abetone, 10
20137 Milano, Italy

Monza
Church of Scientology
Via Nuova Valassina, 354
20035 Lissone, Italy

Novara
Church of Scientology
Via Passalacqua, 28
28100 Novara, Italy

Nuoro
Church of Scientology
Via Lamarmora, 102
08100 Nuoro, Italy

Padua
Church of Scientology
Via Mameli, 1/5
35131 Padova, Italy

Pordenone
Church of Scientology
Via Montereale, 10/C
33170 Pordenone, Italy

Rome
Church of Scientology
Via Sannio N. 64
Zona S. Giovanni-Roma
00183 Roma, Italy

Turin
Church of Scientology
Via Bersezio, 7
10152 Torino, Italy

Verona
Church of Scientology
Corso Milano, 84
37138 Verona, Italy

Netherlands

Amsterdam
Church of Scientology
Nieuwe Zijds Voorburgwal 271
1012 RL Amsterdam, Netherlands

Norway

Oslo
Church of Scientology
Lille Grensen 3
0159 Oslo, Norway

Portugal

Lisbon
Church of Scientology
Rua de Conde Redondo #19
1150 Lisboa, Portugal

Russia

Moscow
Hubbard Humanitarian Center
Prospect Budyonogo 31
105275 Moscow, Russia

Spain

Barcelona
Dianetics Civil Association
C/ Pau Clarís 85, Principal dcha.
08010 Barcelona, Spain

Madrid
Dianetics Civil Association
C/ Montera 20, Piso 1º dcha.
28013 Madrid, Spain

Sweden

Göteborg
Church of Scientology
Odinsgatan 8, 2 tr.
411 03 Göteborg, Sweden

Malmö
Church of Scientology
Porslingsgatan 3
211 32 Malmö, Sweden

Stockholm
Church of Scientology
Götgatan 105
116 62 Stockholm, Sweden

Switzerland

Basel
Church of Scientology
Herrengrabenweg 56
4054 Basel, Switzerland

Bern
Church of Scientology
Muhlemattstr. 31, Postfach 384
3000 Bern 14, Switzerland

Geneva
Church of Scientology
Route de Saint-Julien 7–9
C.P. 823
1227 Carouge
Genève, Switzerland

Lausanne
Church of Scientology
10, rue de la Madeleine
1003 Lausanne, Switzerland

Zurich
Church of Scientology
Badenerstrasse 141
8004 Zürich, Switzerland

Australia

Adelaide
Church of Scientology
24–28 Waymouth Street
Adelaide, South Australia 5000
Australia

Brisbane
Church of Scientology
106 Edward Street
Brisbane, Queensland 4000
Australia

Canberra
Church of Scientology
43–45 East Row
Canberra City, ACT 2601
Australia

Melbourne
Church of Scientology
42–44 Russell Street
Melbourne, Victoria 3000
Australia

Perth
Church of Scientology
108 Murray Street
Perth, Western Australia 6000
Australia

Sydney
Church of Scientology
201 Castlereagh Street
Sydney, New South Wales 2000
Australia

Church of Scientology
Advanced Organization Saint Hill
  Australia, New Zealand and Oceania
19–37 Greek Street
Glebe, New South Wales 2037
Australia

Japan

Tokyo
Scientology Tokyo
1-23-1 Higashi Gotanda
Shinagawa-ku
Tokyo, Japan 141

New Zealand

Auckland
Church of Scientology
159 Queen Street
Auckland 1, New Zealand

Africa

Bulawayo
Church of Scientology
Southampton House, Suite 202
Main Street and 9th Ave.
Bulawayo, Zimbabwe

Cape Town
Church of Scientology
St. Georges Centre, 2nd Floor
13 Hout Street
Cape Town 8001
Republic of South Africa

Durban
Church of Scientology
57 College Lane
Durban 4001
Republic of South Africa

Harare
Church of Scientology
PO Box 3524
87 Livingston Road
Harare, Zimbabwe

Johannesburg
Church of Scientology
6th Floor, Budget House
130 Main Street
Johannesburg 2001
Republic of South Africa

Church of Scientology
1st Floor Bordeaux Centre
Gordon and Jan Smuts Ave.
Blairgowrie, Randburg 2125
Republic of South Africa

Port Elizabeth
Church of Scientology
2 St. Christopher Place
27 Westbourne Road Central
Port Elizabeth 6001
Republic of South Africa

Pretoria
Church of Scientology
306 Ancore Building
Jeppe and Esselen Streets
Pretoria 0002
Republic of South Africa

Argentina

Buenos Aires
Dianetics Association of Argentina
1769 Santa Fe Avenue
Buenos Aires, Argentina

Colombia

Bogotá
Dianetics Cultural Center
Carrera 30 #91–96
Santa Fé de Bogotá
Bogotá, Colombia

Mexico

Guadalajara
Dianetics Cultural Organization, A.C.
Ave. de la Paz 2787
Fracc. Arcos Sur
Sector Juárez, Guadalajara, Jalisco
C.P. 44500, México

Mexico City
Dianetics Cultural Association, A.C.
Carrillo Puerto
54 Bis Colonia Coyoacán
C.P. 04000, México, D.F.

Institute of Applied Philosophy, A.C.
Calle Río Amazonas 11
Colonia Cuauhtemoc
C.P. 06500, México, D.F.

Latin American Cultural Center, A.C.
Guanajuato #233
Colonia Roma
C.P. 06700, México, D.F.

Dianetics Technological
  Institute, A.C.
Mariano Escobedo #746
Colonia Anzures
C.P. 11590, México, D.F.

Dianetics Development
  Organization, A.C.
Heriberto Frías 420
Colonia Narvarte
C.P. 03020, México, D.F.

Dianetics Cultural Organization, A.C.
Nicolás San Juan #1727
Colonia del Valle
C.P. 03100, México, D.F.

Venezuela

Caracas
Dianetics Cultural Organization, A.C.
Avenida Principal de las Palmas,
  Cruce Con Calle Carúpano
Quinta Suha, Las Palmas
Caracas, Venezuela

Valencia
Dianetics Cultural Association, A.C.
Avenida 101, 150-23
Urbanización La Alegría
Apartado Postal 833
Valencia, Venezuela

To obtain any books by L. Ron Hubbard which are not available at your local organization, contact any of the following publishers:

Bridge Publications, Inc.
4751 Fountain Avenue
Los Angeles
California 90029

Continental Publications Liaison Office
696 Yonge Street
Toronto, Ontario
Canada M4Y 2A7

ERA DINÁMICA EDITORES, S.A. de C.V.
Nicolás San Juan 208
Colonia Narvarte
C.P. 03020 México, D.F.

NEW ERA Publications
International ApS
Store Kongensgade 55
1264 Copenhagen K, Denmark

NEW ERA Publications UK, Ltd.
Saint Hill Manor
East Grinstead, West Sussex
England RH19 4JY

NEW ERA Publications Australia Pty Ltd.
Level 3 Ballarat House
68–72 Wentworth Ave.
Surry Hills, New South Wales
2000 Australia

Continental Publications Pty Ltd.
6th Floor, Budget House
130 Main Street
Johannesburg 2001
Republic of South Africa

NEW ERA Publications Italia Srl
Via L.G. Columella, 12
20128 Milano, Italy

NEW ERA Publications
Deutschland GmbH
Bahnhofstraße 40
21629 Neu Wulmstorf, Germany

NEW ERA Publications France E.U.R.L.
105, rue des Moines
75017 Paris, France

NUEVA ERA DINÁMICA, S.A.
C/ Acacias 1
28005 Madrid, Spain

NEW ERA Publications Japan, Inc.
5-4-5-803 Nishi Gotanda
Shinagawa-ku
Tokyo, Japan 141

NEW ERA Publications Russia
c/o Hubbard Humanitarian Center
Prospect Budyonogo 31
105275 Moscow, Russia

To obtain any cassettes by L. Ron Hubbard which are not available at your local organization, contact:

Golden Era Productions
6331 Hollywood Boulevard, Suite 1305
Los Angeles, California 90028-6313

ABOUT THE AUTHOR

L Ron Hubbard is one of the most acclaimed and widely read authors of all time. Over 116 million copies of his works have been sold in more than thirty-two languages around the world. One major reason is that his writing expresses a firsthand knowledge of the basics of life and ability—a knowledge gained not by being on the sidelines of life, but by living to the fullest.

"To know life, you've got to be part of life," he wrote. "You must get down there and *look*, you must get into the nooks and crannies of existence, and you must rub elbows with all kinds and types of men before you can finally establish what man is."

He did exactly that. From the open ranges of his home state of Montana to the hills of China, from the frigid coast of Alaska to the jungles of South Pacific islands, whether working with men on explorations or teaching inexperienced naval crews to survive the ravages of a world war, L. Ron Hubbard truly learned what man and life are all about.

Armed with a keen intellect, boundless energy, limitless curiosity and a unique approach to philosophy and science which emphasized workability and practicality over all else, Ron embarked upon his study of life and its mysteries while still in his teens.

Traveling extensively throughout Asia and the Pacific, he studied the wisdom of Far Eastern philosophies yet observed widespread suffering and poverty. If there was such profound wisdom in the East then why all this, he asked.

After returning to the United States in 1929, Ron pursued the study of mathematics and engineering, enrolling at George Washington University. He was a member of one of the first American classes on nuclear physics and conducted his first experiments dealing with the mind while at the university. He found that despite all of mankind's advances in the physical sciences, a *workable* technology of the mind and life had never been developed. The mental "technologies" which did exist, psychology and psychiatry, were actually barbaric, false subjects—no more workable than the methods of jungle witch doctors.

Ron set out to find the basic principle of existence—a principle which would lead to the unification of knowledge and that would explain the meaning of existence itself—something other philosophers had attempted but never found.

To accomplish this, he began to study man in many different settings and cultures. In the summer of 1932, upon leaving the university, he embarked upon a series of expeditions. The first expedition took him to the Caribbean where he examined the primitive villagers of Martinique. Returning to the West Indies a few months later, he studied cultures of other islands, including Haiti and their esoteric beliefs in voodoo; and later he observed the beliefs of the Puerto Rican hill people.

After his return to the United States, Ron began to substantiate the basis of a theory, and in 1937, he conducted a series of biological experiments that led to a breakthrough discovery which isolated the dynamic principle of existence—the common denominator of all life—SURVIVE!

With these discoveries now in hand, through the first weeks of 1938 Ron wrote his findings in a philosophic work entitled "Excalibur." Upon completion of this historical manuscript he allowed others to review the work. The response was dramatic, and more than a few publishers eagerly sought it. But even as the offers arrived, he knew that he could not publish the book as it did not contain a practical therapy. That is not to imply that the discoveries in "Excalibur" were not later used, as all of its basics have been released in other books or materials by Ron.

Much of his research was financed by his professional literary career as a fiction writer. He became one of the most highly demanded authors in the golden age of popular adventure and science fiction writing during the 1930s and 1940s—interrupted only by active service in the US Navy during World War II. Partially disabled at war's end, in the spring of 1945 he resumed his work in earnest at Oak Knoll Naval Hospital in Oakland, California where he was recovering from injuries.

Among the 5,000 naval and Marine Corps patients at Oak Knoll were hundreds of former American prisoners of war liberated from Japanese camps on South Pacific islands. He noticed that the medical staff at the naval hospital were engaged in trying to do something for the ex-POWs who were in terrible physical condition from starvation and other causes.

In an attempt to alleviate at least some of the suffering, Ron applied what he had learned from his researches. He made further breakthroughs and developed techniques which made possible not only his own recovery from injury, but helped other servicemen to regain their health.

During the years that followed, he spent thousands of hours codifying the first-ever workable technology of the mind. Ron had been steadily accumulating notes on his research, in preparation for a book on the subject. To further verify his theories, he set up an office in Hollywood, California where he could work with people from all walks of life. It wasn't long before he was inundated with a variety of public, eager for his help.

By late 1947, he wrote a manuscript outlining his discoveries of the mind. It was not published at that time, but circulated amongst Ron's friends, who copied it and passed it on to others. (This manuscript was formally published in 1951 and is today titled *The Dynamics of Life.*)

In 1948, he spent three months helping deeply disturbed inmates in a Savannah, Georgia mental hospital. "I worked with some of these," he recalled, "interviewing and helping out as what they call a lay practitioner, which means a volunteer. This gave me some insight into the social problems of insanity and gave me further data in my own researches." It also restored sanity to a score of previously hopeless cases and once again proved that his discoveries were applicable to all, no matter how badly off they were.

As word of Ron's research spread, a steadily increasing flood of letters asked for further information and requested that he detail more applications of his discoveries. To answer all these inquiries he decided to write and publish a comprehensive text on the subject—*Dianetics: The Modern Science of Mental Health*. With the release of *Dianetics* on May 9, 1950, a complete handbook for the application of his new technology was broadly available for the first time. Public interest spread like wildfire and the book shot to the top of the *New York Times* bestseller list, remaining there week after week.

Following the release of this phenomenal bestseller, Ron's time became less his own as he was called upon to give demonstrations and provide more information about Dianetics. He launched into further research, keeping the public informed of his latest breakthroughs with lectures and a flood of published bulletins, magazines and books.

As 1950 drew to a close, and in spite of growing demands on his time by tens of thousands of *Dianetics* readers, he intensified research into the true identity of "life energy," which in *Dianetics* he called the "center of awareness," or the "I."

"The basic discovery of Dianetics was the exact anatomy of the human mind," he wrote. "The aberrative power of engrams was discovered. Procedures were developed for erasing them. The amount of benefit to be gained from running half a dozen engrams exceeded anything that man had ever been able to do for anybody in the history of the human race."

"The discovery of what it was that the mind was coating was the discovery of Scientology.

"It was coating a thetan. A thetan is the person himself—not his body or his name, the physical universe, his mind, or anything else; that which is aware of being aware; the identity which IS the individual. The thetan is most familiar to one and all as *you*."

These discoveries formed the basis of the applied religious philosophy of *Scientology*, the study of the spirit in relationship to itself, universes and other life. Through the application of Scientology technology, desirable changes in the conditions of life can be brought about. It incorporates Dianetics, a vital and basic branch of Scientology, and encompasses techniques which raise personal ability and awareness to heights not previously thought attainable.

It was Ron's lifelong purpose to complete his research into the riddle of man and develop a technology that would bring him up to higher levels of understanding, ability and freedom—a goal which he fully achieved in the development of Dianetics and Scientology. Ron always considered it was not enough that he alone should benefit from the results of his research. He took great care to record every detail of his discoveries so that